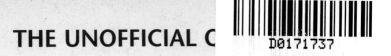

THE UNOFFICIAL G

So You
Think You Know

THE
SIMPSONS?

Clive Gifford

*Hodder
Children's
Books*

a division of Hodder Headline Limited

With thanks to Jim Munson and "Bagpus"

© Hodder Children's Books 2003

This edition published in Great Britain in 2006 by Hodder Children's Books

Editor: Katie Sergeant
Design by Fiona Webb
Cover design: Hodder Children's Books

The right of Clive Gifford to be identified as the author of the work has been asserted by him in accordance with the Copyright, Designs and Patents Act 1988.

10 9 8 7 6 5

ISBN-10: 0340917156
ISBN-13: 9780340917152

Printed by Bookmarque Ltd, Croydon, Surrey

The paper and board used in this paperback by Hodder Children's Books are natural recyclable products made from wood grown in sustainable forests. The manufacturing processes conform to the environmental regulations of the country of origin.

Hodder Children's Books
a division of Hodder Headline Limited
338 Euston Road, London NW1 3BH

Contents

Introduction

So you think you know everything there is to know about the crazy inhabitants of the town of Springfield? Think you can remember all the schemes and plans, pranks and plots? Reckon you can tell Marge's twin sisters apart, can remember all of Bart's bouts of mischief and know all of the regulars at Moe's Tavern? Well, this quiz book will sort you out quicker than you can say, "Mmmm, doughnuts!"

The questions are divided into three levels of difficulty, indicated by a star at the top of each page. One star ★ for easy starter questions (Homer Level), two stars ★★ for medium questions (Marge Level) and three stars ★★★ for a handful of super tough questions (Lisa Level), best only attempted if you reckon you're as smart as Lisa or Database.

Good luck and enjoy!

HOMER
Level Questions

1. What is the name of the youngest member of the Simpson family?

2. What is the name of the mother of the Simpsons?

3. Who is the eldest son of the Simpsons?

4. Do the Simpsons live in Hollyoaks, Springfield or Summer Bay?

5. How many Simpson children are there?

6. What is the name of the father of the Simpsons?

7. What school does Bart attend?

8. What is Homer's favourite drink: cola, beer, wine or tea?

9. Is Mrs Krabappel a teacher, a priest, a store owner or a police officer?

10. In the opening credits, who is usually found writing lines on the blackboard?

11. Does Homer have long black hair, a perm, little hair or is bald?

12. What is the name of the school bus driver?

13. What is the name of Homer's boss?

14. How many sisters does Marge Simpson have?

15. Do Marge's sisters love Homer, loathe Homer or fancy him?

16. What colour is Marge Simpson's hair?

17. What three letter exclamation is Homer famous for often saying?

18. What is the name of the convenience store often featured in *The Simpsons*?

19. Which clown is Bart's hero?

20. What is the surname of Springfield's mayor, beginning with the letter Q?

21. Which boss often says, "Excellent"?

22. Homer has three brothers Al, Bill and Jim: true or false?

23. Into which room do the Simpsons rush in the opening credits?

24. What is the first name of Bart's aunt, beginning with the letter S?

25. What is the colour of Bart's hair?

26. Bart once had to write on the blackboard, "I will not belch the national anthem": true or false?

27. Is Seymour Skinner: Principal of Springfield Elementary School, owner of Springfield TV or the Babysitter Bandit?

28. What is the first name of Bart's aunt, beginning with the letter P?

29. What is the name of the lady who lives next door to the Simpsons?

30. Which member of the Simpsons was once enrolled at the Enriched Learning Centre for Gifted Children: Bart, Lisa or Maggie?

31. Which character frequently adds "diddily" to the end of words?

32. Bleeding Gums Murphy plays the guitar, saxophone or trumpet?

33. Which town, beginning with the letter S, is Springfield's local rival?

34. How many children do the Flanders family have?

35. Which classmate of Bart's is almost always sick: Milhouse, Wendell or Martin Prince?

36. What is the surname of the Reverend in *The Simpsons*?

37. Who has a bet with Homer over their sons' mini-golf competition?

38. Has Marge ever served in the Springfield police force?

39. Kent Brockman is Springfield's local fireman, TV newsreader or postman?

40. What is the name of *The Simpsons* episode first shown at Hallowe'en?

41. The mini-golf competition between Bart and Todd is a victory for Bart, a tie or a victory for Todd?

42. The Simpsons have a thumb on each hand but how many fingers per hand?

43. Barney Gumble can often be found at Moe's Tavern, at the Springfield Speedway or at the Kwik-E-Mart store?

44. Lewis and Richard are friends of Bart's, workmates of Homer's or babies like Maggie?

45. Which one of the following three characters has not been an assistant to Krusty: Sideshow Mel, Principal Skinner or Sideshow Bob?

46. Who hassles Homer when he's working as a Santa in a shopping mall, making him lose his job?

47. To what item in their house do the Simpsons rush in the opening credits?

48. Who is run through a barcode scanner at a checkout in the opening credits?

49. What was the name of the single released and sung by Bart Simpson?

50. In the first full-length episode of *The Simpsons*, which member of the family gets a tattoo?

★   **QUIZ 2**   ★

1. Who is the eldest daughter of the Simpsons?

2. What instrument does Lisa play in the opening titles?

3. Who is older: Lisa or Bart?

4. What is the first name of Grampa Simpson: Al, Abe or Apu?

5. Bart likes to make hoax telephone calls: true or false?

6. Homer works in a fast-food restaurant: true or false?

7. Milhouse is a teacher, friend or cousin of Bart Simpson?

8. Which member of the Simpson family lives in the Springfield Retirement Castle?

9. What is the surname of the Simpsons' neighbours?

10. Are doughnuts, muffins or chocolate biscuits, Homer's favourite sweet snack?

11. Moe, Curly, Ned or Sideshow Bob is the owner of a bar in Springfield?

12. Is Lisa an excellent, average or poor school student?

13. What was the name of the Simpsons' first cat that was run over?

14. Who filled Groundskeeper Willie's house with creamed corn?

15. What sort of creature was TV star, Poochie?

16. Which famous soul singer appeared in an episode of *The Simpsons*: James Brown, Otis Redding or Aretha Franklin?

17. Homer worked on Mr Burns' building sites: true or false?

18. Who phones Moe's Tavern asking if B.O. Problem is there?

19. Marge lets Maggie drive the car in the opening credits: true or false?

20. What sort of creature is Blinky: a fish, a cat, a spider or a bird?

21. What is the name of the Simpsons' family doctor?

22. Which member of the Simpson family becomes a vegetarian after visiting a zoo?

23. Itchy and Scratchy starred in a show with Poochie: true or false?

24. The Springfield school bully is called Nelson, Napoleon, Wellington or Hitler?

25. Mr Burns once tried to marry Marge's mother: true or false?

26. Marge Simpson has webbed feet: true or false?

27. What is the colour of Maggie's hair?

28. Who embarks on a massive public safety campaign after causing the Springfield Nuclear Power Plant to close down?

29. Rod Flanders has one brother: what is his name?

30. Which character most often says, "Okay-dokey", in *The Simpsons*?

31. Elvis Presley was a teacher at Fantasy Rock 'n' Roll Camp: true or false?

32. Grampa Simpson is Homer's dad, Marge's dad or Bart's dad?

33. Does Homer work at a hydroelectric, a coal-fired or a nuclear power plant?

34. Which character nearly always wears earphones, listens to rock music and has long black hair?

35. What country does Apu originally come from?

36. Whose father is the Springfield chief of police?

37. Which close friend of Bart's wears glasses?

38. Whose wife is called Maude?

39. Do Bart and Lisa go to the same school or different schools?

40. Which school bus driver does Bart invite to live in the Simpsons' garage?

41. "Aye carumba" is a catchphrase of which *Simpsons* character?

42. Bart runs over Ned Flanders in the opening credits of the show: true or false?

43. How does Lisa get home in the opening credits of the show?

44. What is the brand of beer, beginning with the letter D, sold at Moe's Tavern?

45. Who gets stuck in the water slide at Mount Splashmore theme park?

46. What does Marge use to dye her hair?

47. Which member of the Beatles sends Marge a thank-you note for her painting of him?

48. To which bar has Bart often made hoax telephone calls?

49. Does Groundskeeper Willie talk with a Scottish, Irish or Mexican accent?

50. What colour hair does Krusty the Clown have?

MARGE
Level Questions

1. Bart makes a deal with God to get his school closed on the day of his history, geography or maths test?

2. What game does the Stonecutters secret society play to celebrate Homer joining them: frisbee, trivial pursuit or ping-pong?

3. Who is fourth grade class president: Bart, Martin Prince, Lisa or Milhouse?

4. Does Herman, Moe or Ned Flanders run a fake jeans business out of the Simpsons' garage?

5. The Capital City Goofball is a mascot for a team playing basketball, baseball or ice hockey?

6. Are the Flanders, the Simpsons or the Van Houtens given $15,000 by the people of Springfield on Christmas Day?

7. Homer buys a thousand springs to turn into merchandise to sell at what event?

8. Does Ned, Moe or Principal Skinner start to date a forgotten actress in the *A Star Is Born* episode?

9. Homer and Bart's model rocket burns down which building in Springfield?

10. After seeing a daredevil show what does Bart try to jump?

11. Who steals 100 pounds of sugar from a crashed lorry and tries to sell it?

12. At the end of the *Lisa The Simpson* episode, Apu turns part of his store into a strip club. What does he call his store?

13. Jebediah is the first name of Homer's dad, the founder of Springfield or Lisa's class teacher?

14. What is the name of the poor part of Springfield where Bart encounters Chester Lampwick: Trampsville, No Hope Central or Bumtown?

15. The Springfield Investorettes start selling what food to battle with Marge's pretzel business: hot dogs, falafels or kebabs?

16. What was the name of Homer's pet lobster: Snappy, Bitey, Blinky or Pinchy?

17. Who sometimes carries a card which reads: "Always do the opposite of what Bart says"?

18. Does Moe, Bart, Barney or Homer see a sign for free beer at a casino and ends up burping up coins?

19. How much does Mr Burns bet a rival baseball team owner that Springfield will win the championship?

20. "I've got some kick-ass seats", is said by Homer to Ned Flanders in a hospital, the courthouse or a church?

21. Questo is a waiter at: The Magic Palace, The Happy Sandwich or The Mystery Meal Diner?

22. What is the name of the new classmate who Milhouse falls in love with?

23. A doll figure of which Springfield character threatens to kill Homer in a *Treehouse of Horror* episode: Krusty the Clown, Mr Burns or Lisa?

24. At the Bloodbath and Beyond gun shop, dangerous applicants for guns are turned away, reported to the police or are limited to three handguns or less?

25. What was the first word that Lisa, as a baby, said: Bart, music, Homer or Mummy?

26. Principal Skinner joins the conga line when the 'Do the Bartman' song is played: true or false?

27. Whose "Down with Homework" t-shirt causes a school riot: Bart, Mrs Krabappel, Milhouse or Lisa?

28. In *Treehouse of Horror V*, Homer goes mad when deprived of beer and TV: true or false?

29. In the episode called *Lisa's Pony*, Apu dates which princess: Kashmir, Calcutta, Nairobi or Mumbai?

30. Homer's fellow inmate at a mental institution, Leon Kompowsky, claims to be which famous pop singer?

31. When Homer doesn't sell the pumpkins he has bought for Hallowe'en he has to borrow money from which characters?

32. What are the gents toilets called at the Rusty Barnacle restaurant?

33. The FBI move the Simpsons away from Springfield to what lake?

34. What is the initial in the middle of Homer Simpson's name?

35. Nana Van Houten is whose grandmother?

36. *King of The Hill* character, Hank Hill, makes a guest appearance in *The Simpsons* to watch his home football team play Bart's. Which team wins?

37. Homer goes on hunger strike when what local sports team threatens to move to Albuquerque: Springfield Isotopes, Springfield Maulers or Springfield Warriors?

38. In a Hallowe'en episode of *The Simpsons*, which famous TV warrior is taken hostage by the Comic Book Guy?

39. Which American Football team does Hank Scorpio give Homer in return for Homer's work?

40. Marge is sent to Traffic School by Chief Wiggum after cutting up what procession in her new car?

41. When posted to a Pacific island to perform missionary work, Homer opens up a casino instead. Was its name the Lucky Savage, the Fortunate Native or the Betcha Primitive?

42. Marge was voted Homecoming Queen, Best Looking Girl or Sports Captain at Springfield High School?

43. Who creates the Angry Dad cartoon that is shown on the Internet?

44. Marge and Homer got married at Shotgun Pete's Wedding Chapel: true or false?

45. Lisa's cellmate in prison is a tattooed lady called Tattoo Annie: true or false?

46. Who writes a letter from Kamp Krusty that ends "Save Us Now!"?

47. What does Homer buy from Bob's RV Roundup: a camper van, a limousine, a satellite television or a doughnut maker?

48. Marge and Homer are found nude inside a windmill, a church or a shopping mall on a mini-golf course?

49. What magazine does Marge read in the supermarket queue in the opening credits?

50. Lisa introduces who to recycling, allowing them to make a fortune?

★ ★   **QUIZ 2**   ★ ★

1. Is Mrs Krabappel married, divorced or has always been single?

2. What three word catchphrase of Bart's involves consuming an item of clothing?

3. Who lost an arm when sticking it out of the school bus window: Martin, Herman, Moe or Nelson?

4. Which member of the Simpson family is photographed in the woods and mistaken for Bigfoot?

5. Which classmate of Lisa's has a crush on her?

6. Dancin' Homer t-shirts go on sale at baseball stadiums for less than $5, less than $25 or less than $100?

7. On Thanksgiving, Christmas Day or the 4th July, does Bart run away and get interviewed by a TV crew?

8. Gabbo is a clown, a ventriloquist doll or a character in an *Itchy & Scratchy* cartoon?

9. Who films Gabbo being rude about his audience to help Krusty return to TV?

10. What is the French first name of the bowling instructor at Bowl-A-Rama: Jean, Claude or Jacques?

11. Which character decides that they want to have their wedding on a trampoline: Barney, Lisa or Mr Burns?

12. Aerosmith and The Red Hot Chili Peppers have played in which Springfield venue?

13. Which classmate does Bart lose a soapbox racer race to: Martin Prince, Milhouse or Jimbo Jones?

14. An instructor in what sport does Marge nearly have an affair with?

15. Homer navigates the raft carrying him and Bart to an oil rig using the smell of chocolate, a burger or corn on the cob as a guide?

16. Which member of the Simpsons is the first to realise the identity of the Springfield Cat Burglar?

17. The Simpsons make sacrifices to pay for the hospital fees for their dog. What does Homer give up?

18. What is the name of Apu's brother: Sanjay, Aziz, Ipu or Phil?

19. Which of these names were not suggestions of Bart's for the new doll Lisa was involved in designing: Wendy Windbag, Ugly Doris, Mouldy Maggie or Loudmouth Lisa?

20. What name does Bart give to his pet elephant: Tusky, Stampy, Heavy or Big Ears?

21. Lurleen Lumpkin is a country and western singer, a blues singer, a hard rock singer or an opera singer?

22. Homer gives $2,000 to his half-brother, his father, his wife or to Mr Burns, to build a baby talk translator?

23. Who runs Kamp Krusty: Mr Burns, Mr Black, Mr Skinner or Mr Brown?

24. What is the name of the giant ape Mr Burns and Smithers catch only for it to break free in New York?

25. Which of the Moe's Tavern regulars takes Homer's car and disappears for two months?

26. Armin Tamzarian spent many years fooling everyone that he was which character in Springfield education?

27. The NRA stands for the National Rifle Association; what did Homer write on his NRA sign instead?

28. Which member of the *Itchy & Scratchy* cartoon team is a cat?

29. Which *Star Trek* actor joins Homer and others on the first trip of the Springfield monorail?

30. Tom becomes Bart's Bigger Brother. Pepi's Bigger Brother was Ned Flanders, Principal Skinner or Homer?

31. How many dollars did Homer get paid when he became a Santa at a shopping mall: $13, $103, $203 or $1,003?

32. What did Bart ask for in the Simpsons' first Christmas on TV: a motorbike, an electric guitar, or a tattoo?

33. Who arranges for the Ramones to play at Mr Burns' birthday party?

34. What was the name the Simpsons gave to their second cat, bought to replace Snowball?

35. Who wishes that Ned Flanders' new store fails and then is guilty when it does?

36. When Bart is imprisoned for the suspected murder of Principal Skinner, is his cellmate: Sideshow Bob, Maude Flanders, Martin Prince or Otto?

37. Homer proposes marriage to Princess Kashmir: true or false?

38. What country does Adil Hoxha, an exchange student, come from: Ukraine, Albania, Turkey or Latvia?

39. Bart tattoos the words "Wide Load" on whose bottom?

40. What colour is the dummy that Maggie usually sucks?

41. Principal Skinner runs Springfield Elementary School but still lives with his mother: true or false?

42. What item, that has been in the Simpson family for six generations, does Santa's Little Helper shred to pieces?

43. 'We're Sending Our Love Down the Well' is a charity single recorded to help which member of the Simpson family in a predicament?

44. At one of Bart's birthdays he receives a voucher for a tango lesson. Does he take the lesson?

45. Which famous scientist makes an appearance in the *They Saved Lisa's Brain* episode: Albert Einstein, Stephen Hawking or Isaac Newton?

46. Who is fired from Homer's musical group, the Be Sharps, for making the group too much like the Village People: Barney, Chief Wiggum, Mr Krabappel or the Comic Book Guy?

47. Does Lisa, Bart, Grampa Simpson or Marge become an active campaigner for non-violent cartoons?

48. Lionel Hutz is hired as a lawyer by whom after a car knocks down Bart: Milhouse, Ned Flanders, Bart or Marge?

49. Apu is the owner of which store in Springfield?

50. What is General Sherman: Krusty the Clown's tank, a giant catfish, Homer's uncle or a regular at Moe's Tavern?

 QUIZ 3 ★ ★

1. What is the nickname given to the criminal, Ms Botz: the Beer Burglar, the Doughnut Desperado or the Babysitter Bandit?

2. What number is Homer when he first joins the Stonecutters: 2, 98, 102 or 908?

3. In *Who Shot Mr Burns Part I*, which Springfield resident struck oil when digging a grave for a dead pet?

4. Maggie calls the police when the rest of her family get into a fight whilst playing what board game?

5. Where does Mr Burns finally get the Loch Ness Monster a job: at a Las Vegas casino, a Paris nightclub or as President of the United States?

6. Who enters the Simpsons' home carrying a shotgun only to be put off by the family's singing: Snake, Jimbo Jones or Sideshow Bob?

7. The Simpsons' car is damaged by a mechanical dinosaur at the Springfield Speedway, the Shelbyville Stadium or Barney's Bowl-A-Rama?

8. Allison Taylor's model scene is sabotaged by Bart who adds a cow's heart, a sheep's eyeball or an old, rotting tomato?

9. Which one of Marge's sisters has no sense of taste or smell?

10. Bart rearranges the words "Cod Platter" to make what words?

11. Which of the following do appear on the *Springfield Squares* TV game show: Homer, Britney Spears, Sideshow Mel, Frank Sinatra or Ron Howard?

12. Shary Bobbins arrives at the Simpsons' house floating down by umbrella: true or false?

13. Does Marge, Mrs Krabappel or Lisa oppose gambling in Springfield only to become addicted to slot machines?

14. What hardware item does Homer use to fasten Maggie's nappy whilst Marge is away?

15. Sideshow Bob planned a gas explosion, a falling piano or a poisoned drink to kill his new wife?

16. What food of Homer's clogs the controls of the Space Shuttle nearly causing disaster?

17. Cirque du Puree is a French circus, a French restaurant or a French range of baby food?

18. Which one of the following characters was not a volunteer fireman trying to save the Simpsons' house: Reverend Lovejoy, Dr Hibbert, Apu or Krusty?

19. Which country launches a massive nuclear attack on Springfield after Mayor Quimby made a joke about them?

20. What job does Laura Powers do at the Simpsons' house: cleaner, babysitter or counsellor?

21. *Simpsons Roasting On An Open Fire* was the title of the first, 50th, 100th or 500th *Simpsons* episode?

22. School Superintendent Chalmers fires Principal Skinner and replaces him with which Simpsons' neighbour?

23. Homer is secretly videotaped complaining about his family during what TV show: *You've Been Exposed*, *The Elevator Files* or *Taxicab Conversations*?

24. Who does Homer's bowling team play in the league championship match: the Gougers, the Holy Rollers, the Stereotypes or the Springfield All-Stars?

25. Who turns out to be the head vampire in a Hallowe'en episode of *The Simpsons*: Marge, Lisa or Ned Flanders?

26. Whose daughter does Bart fall in love with and starts attending Sunday School?

27. *Sumo Babies* is a show featured in the TV guide in one episode: true or false?

28. Who donates blood in order to save Mr Burns' life but is only initially rewarded with a thank-you note?

29. Mulder and Scully from *The X Files* have both made guest appearances on *The Simpsons*: true or false?

30. Famous film director, Martin Scorscese, is replaced on the Springfield Film Festival jury by George Clooney, Brad Pitt or Homer?

31. Who is replaced in the original line-up of the Be Sharps by Barney Gumble?

32. When Homer is a hippie, what does he place in the barrel of Chief Wiggum's gun?

33. Who become the foster parents for Bart, Lisa and Maggie after Bart is found to have head lice?

34. Which character in the show has a wife from India, and has been frequently shot at?

35. What is the name, beginning with the letter F, of the female bully at Springfield Elementary School: Freddie, Fiona or Francine?

36. Bart, Milhouse, Martin and which other boy head to Knoxville in a car Bart hired with fake ID?

37. Can you name the boxing promoter and manager of Dredrick Tatum who has frizzy hair and wears lots of gold jewellery?

38. The Simpsons take a family trip to Bloodbath Gulch just before Grampa is taken ill: true or false?

39. A radioactive rod of plutonium is used as a paperweight at the Springfield Nuclear Plant: true or false?

40. Which of Homer's pals vows to stop drinking after he forgot a birthday party was held for him: Karl, Bill, Lou or Barney?

41. Which doctor tells Homer he has 24 hours to live after eating at a Japanese restaurant?

42. At which poor quality animal theme park does Bart look a lion in the eye which is against the rules?

43. Who makes Homer head of security for the whole of Springfield: Mr Burns, Chief Wiggum or Mayor Quimby?

44. In the shape of what spacecraft was Martin Prince's soapbox racer?

45. Lisa fights to get guns, horror films or alcohol banned only to find Springfield later overrun by zombies?

46. Which two characters decide to write their own episode of *Itchy & Scratchy*?

47. What item does Homer pawn to pay for his family to go into therapy: the deep fat fryer, the family car or the TV set?

48. A Japanese advertising character, which looks just like Homer, is known by what name?

49. A nude Marge and Homer try to escape onlookers by stealing what sort of transport device: a speedboat, a hot air balloon or a tandem bicycle?

50. After getting in trouble with his income tax, Homer works for the FBI and helps uncover a plot by which nuclear plant worker: Karl, Charlie, Smithers or Mindy Simmons?

★ ★   **QUIZ 4**   ★ ★

1. Bart's history test was marked up from an F to what grade: A+, B+ or D-?

2. What is the name of the crime-fighting, talking speedboat found on TV in *The Simpsons*?

3. What is the surname of Springfield's Police Chief: Flanders, Skinner or Wiggum?

4. A spurt of oil from Mr Burns' oil well injures Santa's Little Helper, Homer, Lisa or Milhouse?

5. Homer is offered a job by the owner of the Springfield Isotopes as what?

6. Snake was once a cellmate of Sideshow Bob: true or false?

7. Who proposes an Olympic mascot called Ciggy made up of ashtrays and cigarettes?

8. Homer has a second wife. Did he marry her in Las Vegas, Paris or New York?

9. On what vehicle does Homer attempt to jump the Springfield Gorge?

10. Which member of the *Itchy & Scratchy* show always ends up the victim?

11. Bart sneaks in to the cinema with Jimbo Jones to see: *Space Mutants IV*, *Itchy & Scratchy II* or *Doughnuts: The Movie*?

12. How many babies does Apu's wife, Manjula, have?

13. Whose hair falls out prompting the Simpsons to employ the nanny, Shary Bobbins?

14. Which of the following words or phrases does Homer not usually say: "Mmmm", "Do'h!", "Aye carumba" or "Bart!"?

15. Who buys a trampoline and makes money by charging the local kids $1 a go: Homer, Mr Burns or Milhouse?

16. What is the TV show theme tune that Bart whistles, which annoys Marge?

17. The results of a school aptitude test suggest that Lisa should be a homemaker. What does the test reveal is Bart's ideal job: a spy, policeman, hot dog seller or pop star?

18. A 'nacho hat' is a giant sombrero made of tortilla chips that Homer eats: true or false?

19. What machine that creates cartoons from human movements does Homer invest his family's life savings in?

20. What three-word phrase did Bart write on his test paper to which his teacher marked the paper, "Very poor, even for you"?

21. Bart revives Springfield's dead as zombies but what creature was he trying to bring back from the dead: Blinky, Snowball I or Santa's Little Helper?

22. Springfield riots cause Homer to buy a gun after what boring sports contest between Mexico and Portugal?

23. "Aye carumba" were the first words that Bart said as a baby: true or false?

24. Which of the following landmarks was not in the 'Do the Bartman' video: Great Wall of China, Buckingham Palace, Statue of Liberty or the Berlin Wall?

25. Which former US president moves into a house opposite the Simpsons in the episode, *Two Bad Neighbours*?

26. What colour hair does Jessica Lovejoy have?

27. Homer dresses as Sonny Bono (from Sonny and Cher) to get into a concert by which band: U2, Coldplay or The Red Hot Chili Peppers?

28. The Simpsons get a free trip to Washington as the result of Bart, Lisa or Marge doing well in a Reading Digest competition?

29. Which Springfield resident takes their film to the Oscars but loses out to George C. Scott: the Comic Book Guy, Barney or Mr Burns?

30. Amongst Bart's first spy camera photographs were a picture of his mum shaving her armpits: true or false?

31. After moving out of Springfield for their protection, what name do the Simpsons adopt?

32. The Groovy Grove Natural Farm mainly sells fruit juice, donkey meat, rotten tomatoes or potatoes?

33. When Lisa becomes a vegetarian, what does Homer cook at his next barbecue: a whole roast suckling pig, lettuces or veggie burgers?

34. Hans Moleman turns out to be Bart's real dad: true or false?

35. Who invents an antidote to the nerd scent which attracts bullies?

36. Bart attends the National Grammar Rodeo in Canada: true or false?

37. How many rounds does Homer last against heavyweight champion Dredrick Tatum: one, three, five or fifteen?

38. Wally Kogen turns out to be not Homer's old friend but Mayor Quimby's evil twin: true or false?

39. Bart and Lisa are trapped by a bush fire when taking photographs for the cover of what sort of book: a phone book, a prayer book or a comic book?

40. Who frequently phones Reverend Lovejoy for advice: Captain Lance Murdock, Ned Flanders or Groundskeeper Willie?

41. Maggie fires shots that save Homer from men sent by which criminal: Fat Tony, Tall Ali, or Small Freddie?

42. The *I Married Marge* episode features a flashback to: 1940, 1960, 1970 or 1980?

43. Who wins a bet with Homer over who won the US Presidential election of 1948?

44. What animals are beaten with clubs on Springfield's Whacking Day: snakes, gophers, sheep or rats?

45. Amber Dempsey won which one of these pageant titles: Duff Beer's Little Beauty, Pork Princess or the Damsel of Doughnuts?

46. What is the Ultimate Behemoth: a monster, a camper van, a school bully or Homer's new bowling ball?

47. Which Springfield resident has had a trillion dollar bill in their ownership since World War II?

48. Who gives Bart and Lisa his metal detector to use while Marge and Homer are away: Hans Moleman, Krusty the Clown or Grampa Simpson?

49. What is Maggie's 'price' when she is scanned in the supermarket in the opening credits: $8.63, $84.63, $847.63 or $8400.63?

50. The Reverend Lovejoy's pulpit has alarm, ambulance and disco whistle sound effects to wake up his audience: true or false?

★ ★   **QUIZ 5**   ★ ★

1. Bart receives six, 60 or 600 days detention after he admits to stealing teachers' school-books?

2. Bart took the punishment but who really stole all the teachers' textbooks?

3. At a car show where Homer buys a snow plough, which famous superhero does he see with his vehicle?

4. Does Barney, Hans Moleman or Ned Flanders buy a snow plough and set up a rival business?

5. What object of Homer's sets alight to his house one Sunday morning: a torch, a cigar, a red hot chilli or a travel iron?

6. When Homer sets his house alight, who comes to rescue him?

7. In *Bart To The Future*, Bart sees a vision of life 30 years ahead. What is Bart trying to become?

8. Who is president of the USA at that time: Lisa, Britney Spears or Martin Prince?

9. Is Milhouse, Brad Pitt or Kylie Minogue the President's chief advisor?

10. Is Springfield's TV weather girl called Stephanie, Windy, Sunny or Samantha?

11. Is Stephanie married to Hans Moleman, Kent Brockman or Principal Skinner?

12. When Homer has 24 hours to live he made a list of things to do. What was the first thing on the list?

13. Which one of the following was not on the list: plant a tree, go hang gliding, eat doughnuts or make peace with dad?

14. Was the ninth item on Homer's list: tell-off the boss, go hand gliding or listen to Lisa play her sax?

15. Who plays Marge's husband in the Springfield production of *Oh! Streetcar!*?

16. Is it a crayon, a toothpick or a pair of tweezers found lodged in Homer's brain, which scientists believe is responsible for Homer's lack of intelligence?

17. Which regular at Moe's Tavern first wins the competition to take a trip on the NASA Space Shuttle?

18. Which famous film actor, and star of *The West Wing*, provided the voice for the real Principal Skinner?

19. Does Robbie Williams, Tom Jones or Westlife sing at a romantic meal for Homer and Marge at the Burns' mansion?

20. In *Treehouse of Horror VI*, who is shown as a headless horseman at the beginning of the show: Krusty, Homer, Ned Flanders or Moe?

21. Who was Selma Bouvier's second husband: Troy McClure, Dick Van Dyke or Tom Jones?

22. Which doctor, with the first name Julius, often laughs when he tells patients what is wrong with them?

23. Ned wakes up after drinking with Homer to find himself in a bikini married to Mayor Quimby: true or false?

24. What is the name of the 1970s-loving badly-dressed man with thick glasses: Funky Fred, Disco Stu or Seventies Sam?

25. Mr Burns' old teddy bear was once owned by Adolf Hitler: true or false?

26. How many times has Scratchy killed Itchy: none, eleven or 111?

27. For what sport does Lisa become a goalkeeper for a team run by Apu?

28. Who in Springfield has a suit made out of vampire bat: Comic Book Guy, Rod Flanders or Mr Burns?

29. Where do Martin, Bart and Milhouse stay so that each can keep an eye on their first issue of *Radioactive Man*?

30. In *Treehouse of Horror II*, Homer dreams that who cuts out his brain?

31. Brandine's boyfriend is called: Cletus, Jebediah, Clancy or Godfrey?

32. When Jay Sherman burps, does he turn blue, does food jump off people's plates or does Marge kick him in the shins?

33. Homer accidentally kills Mr Pinchy by giving him a hot bath – what creature is Mr Pinchy?

34. Whose sandcastle of the Taj Mahal did Homer destroy whilst parasailing?

35. Homer bites a cracker shaped like a hippo, lion or giraffe only to find it is made of gold?

36. What is the name of the man who turns out to be Mr Burns' son: Harry, Larry, Barry or Farrell?

37. Homer, covered in roses, falls into his own backyard impressing Marge. What did he fall out of?

38. Whose weight forces the alien spacecraft to fire a second tractor beam to fly away?

39. After discovering he has only four years to live, to which US state do the Simpsons travel to give Homer a rest?

40. Who leaves Grampa Simpson $100,000 in her will: Bea Simmons, Marilyn Monroe or Mrs Krabappel?

41. In *Treehouse of Horror XI*, what vegetable does Homer choke on and die?

42. What is the name of Bart's soapbox racer named after a type of weather: Lil' Lightning, Fast Fury or Storm Raiser?

43. Does Maggie, Lisa or Marge win a series of bets on American Football thus earning the Simpsons lots of money?

44. What nationality is the ice hockey player who gives Lisa his stick after she shows him how to score?

45. Who was the Springfield Nuclear Power Plant union rep before Homer takes on the job: Karl, Barney, Moe or Ned?

46. What is the surname of Bart's schoolmate, Nelson: Putz, Lutz or Muntz?

47. Who finally gets the trillion dollar bill: Fidel Castro, Bill Gates, Tony Blair or Michael Jackson?

48. What substance do Homer and Willie fight over in the school kitchens creating an explosion: gold, plutonium, grease or chocolate?

49. At what Japanese restaurant does it appear that Homer was fatally poisoned: The Happy Sumo, The Hungry Samurai or Tokyo Tom's?

50. Mr Burns is sent to a retirement home for walking around the nuclear plant in the nude: true or false?

★ ★   **QUIZ 6**   ★ ★

1. What is the first name of the babysitter, Ms Botz: Linda, Lisa or Lucille?

2. Members of which TV show, set in a bar, appear in *The Simpsons* episode, *Fear of Flying*?

3. Cooder and Spud ran what stall at the travelling carnival: coconut shy, guess the weight of the baby or ring toss?

4. Who in Springfield has a pet iguana: Selma Bouvier, Milhouse or Chief Wiggum?

5. In *Who Shot Mr Burns Part I*, in what part of his body is Mr Burns shot?

6. In the episode called *They Save Lisa's Brain*, which famous scientist appears to give the Springfield Mensa group a telling-off?

7. What sort of world record does Homer attempt to make after reading the *Duff Book Of World Records*: largest human pyramid, largest doughnut or most doughnuts consumed in an hour?

8. The Be Sharps were a hard rock group, barbershop quartet, jazz band or country and western band?

9. What violent cat and mouse cartoon do many of the children of Springfield love watching?

10. Who leaves prison to marry one of Marge's sisters: Sideshow Bob, Freddy Quimby or Sideshow Mel?

11. Ned Flanders is one of the motorcycle gang called Hell's Satans: true or false?

12. Homer, Moe and Barney urge Bart to kill what sort of creature whilst on a hunting trip: a rabbit, a rare bird, a reindeer or a brown bear?

13. Who goes to the doctors for an eye test and comes out wearing thick black-framed glasses: Jimbo Jones, Krusty the Clown or Bart?

14. Who does Homer carry out of the nuclear power plant in his arms, mimicking a scene in the movie *An Officer and a Gentleman*?

15. Which real life NASA astronaut is part of the Space Shuttle crew along with Homer?

16. Homer becomes a human guinea pig when he loses all his family's money following a visit to a cutting edge cartoon festival: true or false?

17. Who leads a revolt of babies to get their dummies back?

18. In the *Lisa's Sax* episode, what does Homer rub himself with to keep cool?

19. Who develops a big crush on a new neighbour called Laura Powers?

20. In one Hallowe'en episode, massive advertising mascot statues rampage through Springfield: true or false?

21. The first episode of season one was a Christmas, Summer holiday or Easter-based show?

22. Who wins the audition to become Mr Burns' heir: Bart, Smithers, Martin Prince or Otto?

23. Which Springfield resident won the town's Film Festival?

24. Who, along with Bart, unleashes a plague of locusts on former US president George Bush's home?

25. In a *Treehouse of Horror* episode, where is the vampire Mr Burns' castle located: Transylvania, Pennsylvania or Ruritania?

26. Winona Ryder provided the voice for Jacqueline Bouvier, Allison Taylor or Laura Powers?

27. The Gougers are the name of what sort of sports team: baseball, softball or ice hockey?

28. In an episode called *The Springfield Files*, who is almost hypnotised by Homer's wobbling fat?

29. Who opens a left-handed store which eventually fails?

30. What sort of toy does Bart turn Homer into in the *Treehouse of Horror II* episode: a jack-in-the-box, a stuffed teddy bear or a stringed puppet?

31. A fortune-teller tells which Springfield resident that she will fall in love with Hugh Parkfield in the year 2010?

32. From who does Lisa buy an answer sheet to complete a test and get top marks: Martin Prince, Janine Rosberry or Nelson Muntz?

33. What is Principal Skinner's nickname?

34. Lisa invents a robot that can: correct grammar, do all her homework or teach Homer to be a Professor?

35. Which two of the following used to be in the World War II platoon called the Flying Hellfish: Mr Burns, Principal Skinner, Grampa, Troy McClure or Ned Flanders?

36. Belle is the proprietor of Madame Fifi's, the Maison Derriere or the Saucy Salon?

37. From whose Doorbell Fiesta do Marge and Lisa buy a musical doorbell: Madame Bells, Senor Ding-Dong or Herr Ringer?

38. What position does Mary Bailey hold: State Governor, Mayor, Fire Chief or Bank Manager?

39. Who makes a detour in the school bus so that he can propose to his fiancé, Becky?

40. When Grampa Simpson inherits $100,000 what is the first thing he buys: a Rolls Royce, a fez hat, a new apartment or twenty bags of chocolate chip cookies?

41. In *Treehouse of Horror XI*, what sort of creature is Snorky: an elephant, a dolphin or a tiger?

42. Roadkill 2000 is the name of whose soapbox racer: Bart's, Martin's, Nelson's or Homer's?

43. Where does Marge go for a holiday on her own: Rancho Relaxo, The Peachie Beachie or the Slow Down Chalets?

44. What sort of creatures pour out of Lisa's hockey stick causing the Simpsons' home to be badly damaged?

45. Who is Marge's favourite singer: Tom Jones, Elvis, Celine Dion or Sammy Davis Jr?

46. What weapon do Bart and the others use in their war against Nelson and the other school bullies: catapults, water balloons or air pistols?

47. From what country do Homer and Mr Burns paddle their way on a raft after losing a trillion dollars?

48. Who bullies Milhouse into switching dates to the school dance and taking Lisa instead?

49. What Japanese fish does Homer eat at The Happy Sumo, which the chefs think may have poisoned him: cod, blowfish, red snapper or dogfish?

50. For how many dollars did Bart buy an abandoned factory at a tax auction: one, 100, 1000 or 10,000?

★★ **QUIZ 7** ★★

1. What sort of space object does Bart discover whilst helping Principal Skinner on detention: a comet, aliens or a new planet?

2. Who tries to block out all the energy from the sun, and in the same episode is shot by a mystery attacker: Chief Wiggum, Adil Hoxa or Mr Burns?

3. Which classmate of Lisa's once bought her a ticket to the Krusty Anniversary Show?

4. Bart crashes a carnival attraction forcing him and Homer to help out at the carnival. What carnival attraction did Bart crash: Hitler's car, Stalin's bicycle or Churchill's tank?

5. Who is the owner of Advanced Capital Ventures and a member of Springfield's Mensa group?

6. The Ye Olde Off-Ramp Inn has a sign saying: "We're Now Rat-Free", "Two Pizzas For One" or "No Simpsons Allowed"?

7. Who is the male host of *Springfield Action News* and *Eye on Springfield*?

8. The Springfield Mall includes a shop called International House of Answering Machines: true or false?

9. Who teaches Homer to ride his new motorcycle: Moe, Grampa Simpson or Bart?

10. What is the name, beginning with the letter C, of Sideshow Bob's brother: Cecil, Clive or Christopher?

11. Who joins the Junior Campers after drinking a high-sugar drink?

12. Who becomes Lurleen Lumpkin's music business manager?

13. Which of these has not been a store at the Springfield Mall: The Leftorium, Your Name on a Burger or the House of No Refunds?

14. In the *Pokeymom* episode, the Simpsons go to see a rodeo at what institution: a prison, a mental hospital, a school or an old folk's home?

15. Krusty brand products include short-circuiting electric toothbrushes: true or false?

16. What city did Armin Tamzarian originally come from: Capital City, London, Istanbul or Moscow?

17. Which member of the *Itchy & Scratchy* cartoon team is a mouse?

18. In one Hallowe'en episode, Maggie becomes as tall as a skyscraper and takes over the world: true or false?

19. What is the surname of Marge's sisters?

20. What is the name of Apu's wife: Madonna, Meera, Marianne or Manjula?

21. Who gives Homer 10 pounds of shrimp when he complains in a shop: Smithers, Apu or Maude Flanders?

22. What is the first name of former US president George Bush's wife, who becomes the Simpsons' neighbour: Betty, Barbara, Brenda or Britney?

23. What is the name of Mr Burns' long-lost teddy bear: Bobo, Adolf, Jacques or Buck?

24. George Clooney provided the voice of Marge's bowling coach, Jacques: true or false?

25. What country does the Springfield exchange student called Uter come from?

26. Famous basketball player, Magic Johnson, congratulates who after they have saved Springfield from nuclear meltdown?

27. What country does Hugh Parkfield come from?

28. Cesar and Ugolin put anti-freeze into what item that they make: wine, ice cream, chocolate bars or replica Duff's Beer?

29. Which American inventor is Homer inspired by to become an inventor himself?

30. Whose kidneys explode when Homer refuses to stop the car to let them go to the bathroom?

31. In the *Dumbbell Indemnity* episode, what creature comes served wearing a sombrero hat: a shrimp, a chicken, a turkey or a lobster?

32. Whose bulldozer slips a gear and destroys the Maison Derriere?

33. What is the name of the Christian amusement park Ned Flanders creates?

34. What is the "colourful" name of the trucker who beats Homer in a steak-eating contest but then dies of beef poisoning?

35. From which force did the soldiers of the Flying Hellfish liberate some works of art?

36. How many eyes does Blinky have?

37. Lisa sews a likeness of a saxophone player on to the family quilt. Who is it of?

38. Homer becomes an illegal sugar trader after who gets sugar banned from Springfield: Maude Flanders, Martin Prince or Marge Simpson?

39. Lisa frees a turtle, dolphin or lobster that starts a revolution against humans?

40. What colour hair does the school bully, Nelson Muntz, have?

41. What sort of creature is Mr Teeny: a cat, a dog, a radioactive fish or a monkey?

42. The Simpsons are placed in an old house for a reality TV show based on life in: 1695, 1755, 1895 or 1955?

43. Bart throws Lisa's science project tomato at which member of Springfield Elementary School?

44. Who does Homer believe invented the light bulb: Troy McClure, Albert Einstein or Thomas Edison?

45. What local Springfield blues legend takes Lisa under his wing when she is feeling depressed?

46. Who gets a trained monkey called Mojo to make orange juice and perform other household chores: Mr Burns, Mayor Quimby or Homer?

47. Where does Becky stay after her marriage to Otto instantly crumbles?

48. How much does Mr Burns finally offer the Simpsons after knocking over Bart: $5,000, $50,000 or $500,000?

49. Homer and Marge go to a marriage counselling weekend at Catfish Lake after Homer leers at which female neighbour?

50. What is the name of the new worker at the Springfield Nuclear Power Plant who declares Homer as his enemy: Frank Grimes, Kirk Van Houten, Troy McClure or Lyle Lanley?

1. Lisa, Bart or Homer once had a Little Elves lunchbox?

2. When a comet threatens Springfield, to which family's bomb shelter do the people of Springfield rush for safety?

3. Who awakes with a hangover and hands himself over to the police as the person who shot Mr Burns?

4. Only one of the Simpsons is not converted to the Movementarian cult: who is it?

5. Who swallows spark plugs on the 'How Low Will You Go?' contest?

6. Who is the chairman of Itchy & Scratchy International: Lance Murdoch, Roger Myers, Hans Moleman or Albie Arfdecker?

7. What is the name of Selma Bouvier's pet iguana: Jub Jub, Jig Jag, Zub Zub or Zig Zag?

8. What is the name of the belly dancer Homer dances with on a stag night: June Showers, Princess Kashmir or Silky Sandra?

9. A new toy, Funzo, is programmed to do what to other toys?

10. The Collectibles Store owner who saves Homer, Bart, Moe and Barney from a herd of reindeer is called: Cecil, John, Disco Stu or Gerhart?

11. In the episode where Springfield legalises gambling, Bart starts running a casino in the church, his treehouse, Apu's store or at school?

12. Bart smashes his school class' fish tank with what toy: a racing car, skateboard, yo-yo or a computer game console?

13. Bart decides he wants to become a heavy metal guitarist after seeing which band: Aerosmith, Spinal Tap, Iron Maiden or Nickelback?

14. A carbon rod becomes a national hero for saving a space mission and is featured on the cover of *Time* magazine with the headline, "In Rod We Trust": true or false?

15. Who becomes a department store Santa Claus but bets all his earnings away?

16. Who wins the Little Miss Springfield beauty pageant: Mary Shinner, Ann McDermott, Julia Simms or Amber Dempsey?

17. Which character, on finding that everyone in Springfield is dead, dances naked in the church and eats cinemagoers' snacks: Otto, Homer, Todd Flanders or Nelson Muntz?

18. Who does Laura Powers tell Bart she is dating: Krusty, Jimbo Jones, Mayor Quimby or Milhouse?

19. In *King-Size Homer*, what vehicle does Homer steal to travel to and save the nuclear power plant: a police car, an ice cream van or Bart's skateboard?

20. Who takes over the comic book store with Bart when the Comic Book Guy goes to hospital?

21. The weight of what bathroom item forces Mr Burns to sink in his bath and have a near-death experience: a set of scales, a plush bath robe, a bar of soap or a sponge?

22. At Fantasy Rock 'n' Roll Camp, Homer met two members of the Rolling Stones, the Beatles or Coldplay?

23. Evelyn Peters invites which Springfield resident to her exclusive country club: Maude Flanders, Lisa Simpson, Mrs Krabappel or Marge Simpson?

24. For what item does Homer sell his soul to the devil?

25. Roger Myers Sr is the founder of Kwik-E-Mart, the Shelbyville Department Store or Itchy & Scratchy International?

26. Which school child wears lederhosen?

27. *Fiends Reunited* – the new talk show for devils – is a show watched by Lisa and Marge in one episode: true or false?

28. Does Mr Burns buy the Simpsons a rare ancient statue, a bottle of wine or a new car to thank them for his blood transfusion?

29. What was the first word that Maggie said: Mummy, Daddy, dummy or Lisa?

30. In the episode *Lisa's Wedding*, which band are playing a Steel Wheelchair Tour?

31. Which of the following were not a member of the Be Sharps: Apu, Jimbo Jones, Principal Skinner or Ned Flanders?

32. A six-legged chair and what automated tool did Homer invent, leave at a museum and let other people make money from?

33. Who twice escapes the operating room when they should be donating a kidney to Grampa Simpson?

34. Who cooks baked beans in closed cans on the barbecue to keep the flavour in: Apu, Bart, Moe or Homer?

35. What is the first name of Milhouse's father: Kirk, Kris, Karel or Ken?

36. Ned Flanders' amusement park features a statue in front of which miracles appear to occur. What is the statue called?

37. At what religious time of year do the Simpsons fall asleep in church and start dreaming of starring in Bible stories?

38. Does a bear, moose, gorilla or kangaroo wander into Mayor Quimby's office upsetting him so much that he calls for deportation of all illegal immigrants?

39. What is the first name of Homer's boss, Mr Burns?

40. Marge tells the children how her and Homer met, when the TV breaks down, when they're on a holiday walk or on a car journey to Capital City?

41. Professor Lombardo is a Professor of medicine, art, music or philosophy?

42. Why does Homer stop talking and become a good listener to his family?

43. Which rock band comes to the aid of Springfield, split into two by different telephone codes: The Strokes, The Thrills, Aerosmith or The Who?

44. Who wins an award for his episode of *Itchy & Scratchy* presented by Brooke Shields: Martin Prince, Todd Flanders, Freddy Quimby or Grampa Simpson?

45. Who invents a flaming cocktail that mixes alcohol with cough syrup: Homer, Principal Skinner, Bart or Otto?

46. Who do the Simpsons move in with after finding Lenny's house too noisy: the Comic Book Guy, Otto, Jerry Springer or Barney?

47. Dr Monroe wires up the Simpsons for sound, to check their temperature or so that they can use electric shocks on each other?

48. The *Krusty the Clown* show is found on Channel 2, Channel 6, Channel 9 or Channel 12?

49. In whose garden is Otto and Becky's wedding held: the Flanders', the Simpsons' or the Lovejoys'?

50. In the joke spin-off TV show, *Chief Wiggum P. I.*, who is Wiggum's sidekick, known as Skinny Boy: Ralph Wiggum, Milhouse or Principal Skinner?

1. Ashley Grant babysits Bart and Lisa when Marge and Homer visit a marriage counsellor, a candy trade show or Sideshow Bob in jail?

2. Bart re-shapes Principal Skinner's weather balloon so that it looks like Skinner baring his bottom: true or false?

3. Dr Pryor is Homer's doctor, the school psychologist or Marge's ex-boyfriend?

4. Who was Mr Burns struggling with over candy when he was shot: Maggie, Smithers, Homer or Bart?

5. After crashing their camper van, which Simpson is adopted by bears?

6. Which neighbour of the Simpsons is also nicknamed Study Buddy and Toddsky?

7. What creature attacks the plane carrying the Simpsons from Japan to Springfield: a komodo dragon, King Kong or Godzilla?

8. What is the name of the man who operates Gabbo: Hans Moleman, Roger Myers, Arthur Crandall or Alfred Bukofski?

9. Is Moe, Troy McClure or Groundskeeper Willie hired to kidnap the Simpsons back from the Movementarian cult?

10. Who gets their tongue caught in the electric mixer whilst it's still running?

11. Homer and Bart get sent to a leper colony that is based in Hawaii, Fiji, Australia or New Zealand?

12. Handsome Pete is: a clown, a regular at Moe's Tavern, a member of the Springfield mafia or a tenpin bowling coach?

13. After babysitting for the Flanders who is Lisa asked to babysit next?

14. What animal has Lisa always wanted: a pony, snake, a dog or a dolphin?

15. Who claims that their first act if elected mayor would be to kill the entire population of Springfield?

16. Which James Bond actor played the voice of a computer in a *Treehouse of Horror* episode?

17. Whose surname is Nahasapeemapetilon?

18. Is Bart's pet elephant: a real-life Indian elephant, a giant robot elephant, a real-life African elephant or a huge stuffed toy?

19. In the episode where the Simpsons build their own tennis court, which of the following tennis superstars do not appear: Andre Agassi, John McEnroe, Pete Sampras or Tim Henman?

20. The Spine Melter 2000 is a massage chair, a roller coaster ride or a new game at a Springfield arcade?

21. To which city do the Simpsons go to collect their stolen car: Capital City, London, Mexico City or New York?

22. Does Bart, Smithers, Mr Burns or Homer use a matter transporter only to give himself the head of a fly?

23. Who develops a crush on Marge when she starts work at the Springfield Nuclear Power Plant: Karl, Lenny, Mr Burns or Smithers?

24. Lyle Lanley convinces the people of Springfield to build a space rocket, a monorail, a Krusty theme park or a new prison?

25. In the *Mother Simpson* episode, what does Homer do to stay at home on a Saturday: pretends he has a cold, walks with a limp, insists on mowing the lawn or fakes his own death?

26. The Happy Sailor, The Sad Shipman or The Saucy Sailor was the name of the tattoo parlour Bart visited to have a tattoo?

27. Which of the following are actual parts of the Itchy & Scratchy theme park: Friendship Land, Torture Land, Poisonous Cola Land or Explosion Land?

28. Bart is employed by Fat Tony as, a bar tender, pianist, security guard or cleaner at the Legitimate Businessman's Social Club?

29. Who, along with Homer, wakes up after drinking in Las Vegas to find they had both married cocktail waitresses?

30. To which country is Bart sent after causing an explosion that blows Mrs Skinner off the toilet: Germany, Canada, France or Australia?

31. What scientific subject does Homer study at Springfield University: nuclear physics, the chemistry of doughnuts, the biology of turtles or robotics?

32. Bill is the name of one of the KBBL 102.5 radio station disc jockeys whose number one fan is Homer. Is Bill's disc jockey partner: Marty, Monty, Luann or Lyle?

33. Lisa calls off her wedding with Hugh Parkfield in 2010 when he: says they will never see her family again, hits Bart with a cricket bat or gets drunk with Homer in Moe's Tavern?

34. Which parent went to Gudger College and used to be factory manager of Southern Cracker?

35. Uncle Homer's Daycare Centre is opened by Homer after he was injured in hospital. What sport was he playing which caused him to visit the hospital?

36. What is the name of Mayor Quimby's nephew?

37. Which Springfield resident becomes part of the Hullabalooza festival's freak show?

38. In the *Simpsons Bible Stories* episode, who does Marge dream is God: Mr Burns, Mayor Quimby or Ned Flanders?

39. Mrs Krabappel once tried to go out with the drummer from rock band Aerosmith: true or false?

40. Selma runs away and marries Barney Gumble: true or false?

41. Artie Ziff offers Homer how many dollars to spend a weekend with Marge?

42. What creature takes over Santa's Little Helper's doghouse: a porcupine, a hedgehog, a badger or a wolf?

43. Who is released from prison to protect Homer after an attempt is made on his life: Sideshow Bob, Sylvester Stallone or Artie Ziff?

44. Sting appeared as one of the singers on the 'Sending Our Love Down the Well' charity single: true or false?

45. What surprising feature on Stephen Hawking's wheelchair does he use to save Lisa: helicopter blades, a spring-loaded safety net or a rocket jet pack?

46. Homer promises free car washes when he runs for what post in Springfield: Mayor, Police Chief or Sanitation Commissioner?

47. Krusty the Clown had a temporary assistant called Sideshow Rahim: true or false?

48. Which character owns a 1940s Rolls Royce car?

49. Does Lisa, Jayne Greenop or Amber Dempsey develop a crush on the substitute teacher, Mr Bergstrom?

50. Who joins Bart at the military academy provoking much shock: Marge, Lisa, Jimbo Jones or Blinky the fish?

1. 'Old Red' is the name given to which teacher's pen used for grading homework?

2. What is the name of Godfrey Jones' downmarket news show: *Garbage Group*, *Rock Bottom* or *Trash Talk*?

3. Who opens a clown college which Homer decides to attend?

4. Which 'royal-named' classmate of Bart's is the class brainbox?

5. What is the name of Radioactive Man's sidekick: Plutonium Boy, Fallout Boy or Two Heads Boy?

6. What is the name of Springfield's baseball team: the Isotopes, the Gougers or the Maulers?

7. To which country do the Simpsons go on holiday after following Chuck Garabedian's saving tips: Turkey, Ghana, England or Japan?

8. With what part of his body does the injured Lance Murdock use a pen to sign an autograph for Bart whilst in hospital?

9. In *The Last Temptation of Krust*, Krusty is found passed out from too much alcohol on which family's lawn?

10. Lisa saws the head off the statue of the founder of Springfield: true or false?

11. What is the name of the restaurant Homer is spotted at dancing with a belly dancer?

12. At a religious revival meeting, Brother Faith helps Homer to remove a wig, a bucket or a doughnut super-glued to his head?

13. Who faked his own death and went under the name Rory B Bellows to avoid paying tax: Mr Burns, Roger Myers or Krusty the Clown?

14. Who gets drunk accidentally at the St Patrick's Day Parade causing Mayor Quimby to ban all alcohol in Springfield: Mrs Krabappel, Bart or Maude Flanders?

15. Aristotle Amadopolis is the owner of a rival nuclear power plant but in which town?

16. Smithers is the personal assistant of which Springfield character?

17. Are Ernst and Gunter: lion tamers, used-car salesmen or casino croupiers?

18. David Beckham becomes Bart's best friend in a year 2000 episode of *The Simpsons*: true or false?

19. Does Ned Flanders, Chief Wiggum or Barney give Homer a ticket to the American Football, and arrange for the ball used in the game to be given to him as a gift?

20. Which tennis star does Homer change their last name to Simpson, to play with him in a tennis doubles tournament?

21. Bart sold a ticket to ride on what vehicle to pay for Lisa to enter the beauty pageant: an airship, a helicopter, a speedboat or the Space Shuttle?

22. What is the name of the mountain where Barney gets trapped under an avalanche: Widow's Peak, Old Lumpy, Jebediah's Peak or Mount Burns?

23. Who is found to be a witch in the Sprynge-Fielde of 1649?

24. Which family member of the Simpsons has stayed underground for 25 years after raiding a germ warfare lab run by Mr Burns?

25. Doris, the lunchlady at Bart and Lisa's school, has served meat from a tin labelled "horse parts": true or false?

26. Which of these rock stars does Homer not meet at Fantasy Rock 'n' Roll Camp: Tom Petty, Keith Richards, Ozzy Osbourne or Elvis Costello?

27. Which divorced lady did Marge form a friendship with after going to the ballet together: Nicole Kidman, Bea Simmons or Ruth Powers?

28. Searing Gas Pain Land is a real part of the Itchy & Scratchy theme park: true or false?

29. Rod and Todd Flanders dress up as what animal for one Hallowe'en episode of *The Simpsons*: wolves, vultures, sheep or bears?

30. In one episode, Homer is placed in the New Bedlam Rest Home for the Emotionally Interesting: true or false?

31. Mr Burns steals the Simpsons' dozens of puppies in order to make a suit out of them: true or false?

32. From which character in prison does Bart receive a threatening letter written in blood: Sideshow Mel, Krusty the Clown, Nelson Muntz or Sideshow Bob?

33. Bart accidentally kills what type of bird when he uses Nelson's BB gun: an albatross, a robin or a bald eagle?

34. In what city does Homer teach Ned Flanders how to drink and gamble?

35. In *The Boy Who Knew Too Much* episode, which member of the Simpson family tells the truth and is rewarded with four months detention?

36. What do Nelson, Jimbo, Dolph and Kearney throw at Principal Skinner's house: tomatoes, small puppies, out-of-date coleslaw or stones?

37. In the *Simpsons Tall Tales* episode, Bart is shown as which character in the tales of Tom Sawyer and Huck Finn?

38. Whose stomach is capable of stopping a fired cannon ball: Barney's, Lenny's, Karl's or Homer's?

39. When Lisa dreams of being an Israelite slave, who does she dream of as Moses: Bart, Homer, Milhouse or Hans Moleman?

40. Who did Marge go the school prom with in 1974: Homer Simpson, Artie Ziff, Kent Brockman or Krusty the Clown?

41. The workplace of which member of the Simpsons is shown in the opening credits of many early episodes?

42. Which ex-date of Marge's returns to Springfield in a helicopter and invites the Simpsons to his yacht?

43. At the Festival of Books which Lisa takes Bart and Homer to, which Springfield TV favourite is signing books: Krusty, Troy McClure or Radioactive Man?

44. Mr Burns sell his nuclear power plant for $100 million to a company from what European nation?

45. Who is King of the Mardi Gras only to find that his float has been sabotaged to crash?

46. "We put the fun in funerals" is the slogan of a Springfield funeral home: true or false?

47. Who does Bart label the "Human Punching Bag" when playing video boxing?

48. When Springfield develops a terrible rubbish problem, what do the town's people decide to do?

49. In the popular Springfield TV series *McBain*, who is McBain's arch-enemy: Senator Mendoza, Congressman Fitz or President Jackson?

50. In the *Beyond Blunderdome* episode, which famous movie star agrees with Homer's views on a film and makes him a Hollywood consultant: George Clooney, Mel Gibson or Brad Pitt?

1. Homer steals a rare gummy candy at a show. Was it in the shape of the Venus de Milo, the Mona Lisa or Michael Jordan?

2. Don Vittorio is the owner of the Gougers hockey team, head of the local mafia or the leader of the Stonecutters?

3. Who fires people for not enjoying themselves on the company picnic?

4. Where do Patty and Selma work: the Springfield Nuclear Plant, Kwik-E-Mart or the Department of Motor Vehicles?

5. Who shows Bart the Zen way of concentration so that he can improve his mini-golf play: Lance Murdoch, Bruce Lee, Jackie Chan or Lisa?

6. In Japan, Homer throws which Japanese dignitary into a container for soiled Sumo thongs?

7. Luke Perry is fired out of Krusty's cannon and into a pillow factory: true or false?

8. Which restaurant has a sign with a steak singing into a microphone?

9. Who do both Grampa Simpson and Mr Burns court in the same episode: Mrs Bouvier, Angie Dickinson, Barbara Streisand or Mrs Krabappel?

10. Which US talk show host does Bart convince to let Krusty on a stand-up comedy bill?

11. Mr Burns' yacht is called: The Plutonium Princess, Gone Fission or The Atomic Sailor?

12. Lisa reveals that Springfield's founder, Jebediah Springfield, was: a woman, a pirate, an American Civil War hero or a German spy?

13. All Creatures Great and Cheap is a pet shop visited by Homer to buy Lisa what creature: a lizard, a pony or a hamster?

14. Who is Bart cast adrift with on the open sea after a raft trip goes wrong?

15. In the episode when Krusty the Clown's TV show was cancelled, who was not a guest star: Bette Middler, Elizabeth Taylor, Ronan Keating or Luke Perry?

16. After giving his relatives their inheritance, where does Grampa Simpson get a job: the Leftorium, Krustyburger or the Kwik-E-Mart?

17. Who gives Bart his elephant prize: Bill and Marty, Mr Burns or Mr Blackheart?

18. Dirt First is a group joined by Lisa, Moe, Bart or Marge?

19. Serena Williams partners Marge in a doubles tennis tournament: true or false?

20. What is the name of the summer camp Bart wants to go on: Camp Carumba, Vandal's Village or Kamp Krusty?

21. In which city did Homer, as a young man, have his wallet stolen by a policeman and Woody Allen empty a rubbish bin over him?

22. Who is the only child in Springfield who, as a punishment, does not see the new *Itchy & Scratchy* movie?

23. Aunt Glady's pet, adopted by Selma, was what sort of creature?

24. Which Simpson plays the guitar and was a member of the Springfield Seven: Marge, Lisa, Grampa Simpson or Mother Simpson?

25. At what racetrack did the Simpsons' pet dog used to race?

26. In the Simpsons first ever Christmas on TV, what animal did Lisa request as her Christmas present?

27. Homer's final exam grade at University is changed by the nerds to what mark: E-, D, C+, B or A+?

28. The Simpsons' car loses its roof but gains a US Army missile as they take a short cut to which theme park?

29. Which *Simpsons* character gives his name to a chocolate breakfast cereal: Krusty the Clown, Mayor Quimby, Mr Burns or Bart?

30. Which family has to live in the church basement after finding their house has been destroyed by a hurricane: the Van Houtens, the Flanders or the Simpsons?

31. In the student exchange programme, which Springfield schoolchild is sent to France?

32. What creatures hatch from the 'birds' eggs that Bart looks after: lizards, aliens or crabs?

33. Rainer Wolfcastle is the star of what series of films which are often shown in Springfield?

34. During a teachers' strike who is called in to teach Bart's class: Lisa, Marge, Otto or Robbie Williams?

35. Who asks Gloria out after being inspired by one of Homer's fortune cookies?

36. Who has a crisis and changes the way they act when no one signs their school yearbook: Martin, Lisa, Milhouse or Bart?

37. Wally Kogen gets which famous country singer to let him and Homer out of a jail cell in a Superbowl stadium?

38. Lisa gets the Red Sea to part by getting all the nearby toilets flushed: true or false?

39. When Homer is promoted he employs a personal assistant. Is he called Karl, Lyndon, Anthony or William?

40. Which famous religious figure turns up for the launch of Homer's new motor car: the Dalai Lama, the Pope or the Archbishop of Canterbury?

41. What is the name of Rainer Wolfcastle's daughter who develops a crush on Bart: Greta, Jenna or Hannah?

42. Where does Bart throw his Superstar Celebrity microphone to play a practical joke?

43. After being cursed by a gypsy, what half of an animal does Lisa turn into?

44. Which president appears in an episode claiming that Homer is louder than World War II: Ronald Reagan, Bill Clinton or George Bush?

45. Which of the following films did Troy McClure not star in: *Dig Your Own Grave and Save*, *Suddenly Last Supper*, *Be-Bop Idol* or *Gladys The Groovy Mule*?

46. An out-of-shape Homer joins a gym. Who starts training him?

47. How much does Mr Burns first offer Homer to pay for the injuries to Bart: $100, $1,000 or $10,000?

48. Who does Lisa call a baboon after embarrassing her at the Springfield museum?

49. During the ban on alcohol in Springfield, which policeman is replaced by Rex Banner from Washington?

50. Lisa gets an archaeological survey on a site of a forthcoming shopping mall. What is the name of the meadow site: Mammoth Glades, Angel Fields or Sabertooth Meadow?

★★   **QUIZ 12**   ★★

1. Who is about to marry Marge's mum when he kicks Bart for dropping the wedding ring: Mr Burns, Roger Myers, Chief Wiggum or Mayor Quimby?

2. What is the name of Fat Tony's mafia boss?

3. Which classmate of Lisa's has an imaginary friend who sometimes tells him to start fires: Amber Dempsey, Jimbo Jones or Ralph Wiggum?

4. What jobs do the Simpsons get in Japan to pay their way back to Springfield?

5. Bart and Lisa discover an old record with Homer's, Marge's or Mr Burns' face on the cover?

6. What is the colour of the dress Ned is forced to wear whilst mowing the Simpsons' lawn after losing a bet?

7. Which member of the Simpson family invents a love-making potion which Homer and Grampa go into business to sell?

8. After reinventing himself, Krusty finally sells out to advertise what item: a new car, a new soft drink or a new brand of handgun?

9. Who sawed off the head of the statue of Jebediah Springfield: Jimbo Jones, Bart, Milhouse or Nelson?

10. In the episode where the Simpsons are entrusted with Mr Burns' mansion, which famous female pop singer makes an appearance: Kylie Minogue, Jennifer Lopez or Britney Spears?

11. Who is the president of the Springfield Historical Society: Holliss Hurlbut, Ned Flanders, Principal Skinner or Lunchlady Doris?

12. To put off sexy thoughts of a co-worker, which of his friends does Homer imagine in a bikini: Karl, Lenny or Barney?

13. Lurleen Lumpkin worked at the Beer N' Brawl, The Lonesome Cowboy or the Lassoo Inn?

14. Smithers is the owner of a large collection of: potato chips of the world, Malibu Stacy dolls or postage stamps?

15. Who does Mr Burns promote to Executive Assistant in Charge of Hi-Jinks: Smithers, Bart, Karl or Homer?

16. Homer partners Bjorn Borg in a tennis doubles match: true or false?

17. According to Bart, what numbers were missing from his Krusty brand electronic calculator?

18. Sergeant Seymour Skinner was sold into slave labour in China, Scotland, Vietnam or Canada?

19. Which singer, kidnapped by Mr Burns, is seen performing at the Copper Slipper in Las Vegas: Robbie Williams, Tom Jones or Michael Jackson?

20. Sideshow Bob threatens to detonate a nuclear bomb unless Springfield abolishes: prisons, doughnuts, television or schools?

21. Who was Selma Bouvier first married to: Krusty the Clown, Homer Simpson or Sideshow Bob?

22. Which lady advises Marge to have plastic surgery which results in Marge having new breasts?

23. Which character is electrocuted by a solar-powered electric chair: Snake, Kirby or Todd Flanders?

24. Who becomes attached to Mr Burns' old teddy bear forcing Mr Burns into attempts at threatening and stealing?

25. Birch Barlow is a hippie, a radio talk show host or a member of Fat Tony's criminal gang?

26. Rabbi Krustofski is the father of which character in the show?

27. Bart has his appendix taken out after eating a Krusty-O cereal which was: vanilla instead of chocolate flavour, made of metal or part of a horse?

28. What colour is Krusty's nose?

29. In *Treehouse of Horror IX*, whose hair is transplanted on to Homer's head making him kill Moe and Apu: Snake's, Freddy Quimby's or Sideshow Bob's?

30. Which Springfield child gets a starring role in the *Radioactive Man* film: Bart, Lisa, Amber Dempsey or Milhouse?

31. Who danced around nude in a candy floss machine at the Springfield Chilli Cook-Off?

32. Waylon Sr was the father of which *Simpsons* character and employee of Mr Burns?

33. Which of the following items have become Krusty the Clown merchandise: pyjamas, electric toothbrushes, mobile phones, cough syrup or cattle prods?

34. Rupert Murdoch has Homer and his friends ejected from his luxury box at what sporting occasion: the Olympics, the World Cup Soccer Finals or the Superbowl?

35. Who does Bart fight in the dream of being David fighting Goliath II?

36. Which of the following is not on a tombstone in the Springfield cemetery: Your Name Here, Not So Crazy Horse, Elvis or Garfield?

37. Bea Simmons has a crush on which member of the Simpson family?

38. Over which girl do Bart and Milhouse have a fight in Canada: Allison Powers, Greta Wolfcastle or Astrid Weller?

39. Millicent is a posh instructor at an art school, a music school or a horse stables?

40. Smooth Jimmy Apollo makes predictions on American football, horse-racing, tortoise-racing or baseball?

41. In *Treehouse of Horror XII*, Bart battles a Harry Potter-styled Mr Burns and Smithers. What is Smithers' name in these scenes?

42. Dr Wolfe gives Lisa: an artificial leg, ugly glasses, ugly teeth braces or a new heart?

43. Which Springfield doctor believes that actor Larry Hagman has three hearts?

44. After how many bouts of video boxing does Bart retire as undefeated champion: 28, 38, 48 or 58?

45. What is the name of Springfield's tallest mountain which Homer attempts to climb: Mount Burns, Widow's Peak or the Murderhorn?

46. How many eyes do the aliens Kodos and Kang have?

47. What is the name of the doctor that testified to Bart's fake injuries in court: Dr Monroe, Dr Riviera or Dr Hibbert?

48. How much do Bart, Milhouse and Martin pay for a first issue of *Radioactive Man*: $1, $10, $100 or $1,000?

49. In whose playhouse is Bart shocked to see Mrs Krabappel and Principal Skinner kiss?

50. The skeleton of an angel, a sabertooth tiger, a unicorn or a giant lizard is found at Sabertooth Meadow?

★★ **QUIZ 13** ★★

1. Luann is the mother of which schoolmate of Bart's: Milhouse, Martin Prince or Rod Flanders?

2. In the second episode of *The Simpsons*, Bart was imprisoned, joined the band Nirvana or was labelled a child genius?

3. Homer re-mortgages his house to buy the Ultimate Behemoth: true or false?

4. When Homer is banned from Moe's Tavern, to which transport terminal does he head to start drinking: the docks, the airport or the bus station?

5. To what big city do the Simpsons move when Homer is offered a baseball job?

6. Is Wendell a classmate of Bart's, a classmate of Lisa's or a work colleague of Homer's?

7. Which sidekick of Krusty the Clown plays the slide whistle?

8. Which former US President takes part in Whacking Day at Springfield: Bill Clinton, Richard Nixon or Abraham Lincoln?

9. Who moves into Bart's treehouse after being kicked out of the family home: Homer, Ned Flanders or Milhouse?

10. In *Dumbbell Indemnity*, Moe starts dating a flower seller. Was her name: Daisy, Iris, Renee or Flora?

11. Who owns the Bowl-A-Rama bowling alley: Mr Burns, Apu, Moe or Barney?

12. Which long-dead famous person from Springfield turns out to have had a silver tongue?

13. U2 have appeared on *The Simpsons*: true or false?

14. Is Brad Goodman, Jeff Hapman or Nick Riviera the name of the self-help guru whose video is called, "Adjusting Your Self-o-Stat"?

15. What is Bart's catchphrase when he becomes famous for working with Krusty the Clown?

16. Lou and Eddie are school bullies, Springfield policemen or members of Homer's bowling team?

17. In one episode, Ned Flanders hires Fat Tony to kill the Simpsons with rubber clubs: true or false?

18. What sort of zoo creature does Mr Burns convince Homer to dress up as in the *Homer vs. Dignity* episode: an elephant, a panda or a hippo?

19. Who does Sideshow Bob hypnotise and strap with dynamite in an attempt to blow up Krusty the Clown: Bart, Homer, Lisa or the Reverend Lovejoy?

20. Marge meant to order weight loss cassette tapes for Homer but what arrived instead: word-improving tapes, confidence-improving tapes or how to be a better parent tapes?

21. Who tells a scary tale of Mr Burns and Smithers trying to catch a giant ape?

22. The Reverend Lovejoy is seen dancing with the devil during which song sung by Bart: 'Deep, Deep Trouble', 'Do the Bartman' or 'Bart's Big Blues'?

23. Who buys Professor Frink's matter transporter in a sale?

24. Which doctor will perform many operations for just $129.95?

25. Does Sideshow Bob, Ramim, Apu or Mr Burns kidnap Bart and fly the Wright Flyer biplane to attack Krusty the Clown?

26. Which enemy of Bart's beats Quimby to become Mayor of Springfield?

27. What was the name of the Simpsons' first cat that was run over: Santa's Little Helper, Snowball, Fluffy or Reg?

28. What martial art class does Bart skip to go to the arcade?

29. What unusual clothing item does Don Vittorio wear: a black cape, a fez hat, a pink ladies dress or a brown leather skirt?

30. Bart won $100,000 in a court case against a cereal company, but how much did he get after legal fees: $500, $5,000 or $50,000?

31. Who duplicates Bart's photo of his dad dancing with a belly dancer?

32. Which character has a tattoo on his chest saying, "Die Bart Die": Sideshow Bob, Nelson Muntz or Smithers?

33. Homer crashes into the weekend home of Alec Baldwin and Kim Basinger when a parasail, limousine or jet ski goes haywire?

34. Bart steps in to the role of Radioactive Man's sidekick after a friend of his quits: true or false?

35. In *The Springfield Files* episode, who turns out to be the alien?

36. Homer breaks his jaw when he runs into a statue of a boxer: true or false?

37. Who do the aliens, Kang and Kodos, question about the Earth's leaders: Homer, Ned Flanders, Bart or Barney?

38. In the *Sunday, Cruddy Sunday* episode, Homer takes home the winning trophy from what sport?

39. Astrid Weller is the owner of what sort of place: a bar, a designer clothes outlet, an art gallery or the new European-styled doughnut store?

40. Which resident of Springfield is given an award for being the town's oldest citizen: Grampa, Hans Moleman or Mr Burns?

41. Which member of school staff proposes marriage to Marge's sister, Patty?

42. Lisa has been phoning which country to check on an orphan she has adopted: Senegal, Brazil, Ecuador or Bangladesh?

43. What colour hair does Groundskeeper Willie have?

44. What type of nut does Mr Burns admit to loving: cashew, walnuts, brazil nuts or hazelnuts?

45. Homer only gets a short way up the Murderhorn mountain. What happens when he fixes his flag to a mountain ledge?

46. Does Jimbo, Dolph or Kearney wear a woolly hat?

47. Which daredevil character has the slogan, "No Stranger to Danger"?

48 Who discovers a radioactive rod down his back in the opening credits of the show: Homer, Bart or Chief Wiggum?

49. What is the name of the party maths entertainer who wears a wizard's robe and hat?

50. Who displays the skeleton of an angel in his garage and charges visitors: Ned Flanders, Homer or Kirk Van Houten?

★ ★   **QUIZ 14**   ★ ★

---

1. What is the name of the doctor who examines Marge and her fear of flying: Dr Dweeb, Dr Zweig or Dr Retard?

2. Number One and Grampa are both members of the Masons, the Springfield Elks, the Stonecutters or the Itchy & Scratchy Adult Fan Club?

3. Which town's children steal Springfield's cherished lemon tree: Shelbyville, Capital City or Grimestown?

4. One of the poor orphans seen in a Christmas *Simpsons* edition was called: Poor Petra, Poor Violet, Poor Daisy or Poor Flora?

5. Homer, Professor Frink, Willie and Mr Burns travel to Scotland to catch what legendary lake creature?

6. In *Treehouse of Horror XIII*, what object of Homer's starts making clones of him: his rucksack, his hammock, his car or his coat?

7. Rock 'n' roller, Little Richard, appears in the episode in which Mrs Krabappel gets engaged to whom?

8. Montymort is a character based on which Springfield resident who appears in a *Simpsons* Hallowe'en episode?

9. When the church sells out to Mr Burns, what religion does Lisa take up: Buddhism, Hinduism or Sikhism?

10. Which female neighbour only reads the Bible?

11. Which new classmate of Lisa's outplays her on the saxophone: Amber Dempsey, Candice Jackson or Allison Taylor?

12. Which member of the Springfield community builds a website offering scandalous news stories and wins a Pulitzer Prize for their efforts: Homer, Reverend Lovejoy or Kent Brockman?

13. Stupidity in the Simpson family is caused by a gene which only occurs in males, only in females or in all Simpsons?

14. Who replaces Smithers as Mr Burns' personal assistant whilst Smithers takes a holiday?

15. On "Go To Work With Your Parents Day", which schoolchild earns $600: Milhouse, Lisa or Martin Prince?

16. At Mr Burns' survival retreat for his employees, what happens to the last team that reach the mountain cabin?

17. When Moe accidentally sets his bar on fire, who saves Moe and Homer after first saving some barrels of beer?

18. Phoney McRingRing is the mascot and president of the local phone company: true or false?

19. What is the name of the boy band featuring Bart and others from Springfield?

20. Colonel Hapablap is a member of the air force, navy or army?

21. Who replaces Otto as a member of Homer's bowling team, the Pin Pals: Mr Burns, Jimbo Jones or Principal Skinner?

22. Eyeball Plucked World is a part of the Itchy & Scratchy theme park: true or false?

23. Does Reverend Lovejoy have a son, a daughter or no children?

24. With whom does Homer perform a cycling trick to have his life spared by criminals: Sideshow Mel, Krusty or Captain Lance Murdock?

25. The Simpsons' houseguest Jay Sherman is a film critic but from which American city: Los Angeles, Washington or New York?

26. Which dying jazz musician does Lisa see in hospital when she visits Bart?

27. Which famous film director and former star of *Happy Days* drops by on Homer, Alec Baldwin and Kim Basinger in Springfield: Henry Winkler, Ron Howard or Peter Jackson?

28. In the *D'Oh-In In The Wind* episode, what does Homer's middle name turn out to be: Jay, Jebediah, Jeremiah or Jennifer?

29. Who sells their soul to Milhouse for $5?

30. Agnes Skinner is Principal Skinner's mother, wife, sister or daughter?

31. Dr Hibbert is worried more about the level of what substance in Homer's blood than his cholesterol level: alcohol, sugar or gravy?

32. Which famous alien detectives visit Springfield to interview Homer about alien sightings?

33. Who becomes the new owner of the Springfield Isotopes baseball team: Duff Beer, Smithers, Grampa Simpson or Mayor Quimby?

34. When Bart steals an army tank, he shoots down a statue in Springfield, a space satellite, a seagull or an airliner?

35. Who, after plastic surgery, gets hired on the TV soap, *It Never Ends*?

36. What is the name of the town the Simpsons move to when Homer gets a job with the Globex Corporation: Capital City, Shelbyville or Cypress Creek?

37. When Homer becomes a professional boxer, who becomes his manager: Don King, Moe, Ned Flanders or Mr Burns?

38. To what name does Homer change his so that he isn't mistaken for the bumbling fool in the *Police Cops* TV show?

39. 'Deep, Deep Trouble' is a song sung by which member of the Simpson family?

40. Homer's mangled barbecue is declared an art sculpture. Who buys it?

41. Bart and Homer's horse, Duncan, is given a makeover as a tough racehorse known by what name: Furious D, Duncan the Devil, Dangerous D or Slam Dunc?

42. Bart shows his classmates Mrs Krabappel and Principal Skinner kissing but in what place were they hiding: the janitor's cupboard, the gymnasium or the principal's office?

43. What is the name of the large cinema complex, beginning with the letter G, often visited by Springfield's residents?

44. Who is kidnapped when the Simpsons head to Rio de Janeiro: Maggie, Marge, Lisa or Homer?

45. Can you name one of the two partners Homer starts up a security company with?

46. Yuk-ingham Palace is a joke shop, a doctor's surgery or an unpleasant looking hotel?

47. Bart and Lisa find a film can near the Aztec Theatre containing a different ending for what old, famous film: *Gone With The Wind*, *Ghostbusters*, *Casablanca* or *Jaws*?

48. What is the name of Krusty the Clown's chimp?

49. Homer has a heart attack when Lisa tears up a cheque from Mr Burns for how many million dollars: two, ten, twelve or fifty?

50. After meeting Lionel Hurtz, Marge becomes a real estate agent but for which company: Red Blazer Realty, Half-Price Housing or Easy Estates Inc.?

★ ★   **QUIZ 15**   ★ ★

1. Who untied Bart and Lisa after they were tied up by their babysitter: Otto, Maggie or Milhouse?

2. In *Homer The Great*, what is the name of the secret society Homer finds Moe, Lenny and Chief Wiggum are a part of?

3. What is the Christmas-based name of the greyhound that Homer and Bart adopt at Christmas time?

4. What radioactive creature does Marge serve Mr Burns when he comes round for dinner: a fish, a duck or a prawn?

5. Bart sets fire to what item when playing with his new remote controlled fire engine on Christmas Day?

6. When Homer is an artist he floods Springfield. Paintings of what Italian city inspired him to do so?

7. Bart learns that he advertised what sort of product as a baby: diapers, mouthwash or baby food?

8. Moe returns from bartending school to revamp his bar and gives it a trendy, single letter name? What is the letter?

9. What is the name of the daredevil who appears at the Springfield Speedway arena?

10. Bart breaks his leg when he tries to jump into what new feature of his family's home: a swimming pool, a Jacuzzi or a sandpit?

11. Does Moe, Lenny or Barney plan a trip to Hawaii with his girlfriend using money from an insurance scam that lands Homer in jail?

12. Which of Marge's sisters wears a blue dress and has a parting in her hair?

13. Princess Kashmir is also known as June Days, April Flowers or May Rains?

14. Which newspaper breaks the story of Selma dating Troy McClure?

15. Which police officer is addicted to doughnuts: McBain, Chief Wiggum or Troy McClure?

16. Who employs Homer as a blackjack dealer at a new casino: Moe, Mr Burns, Grampa Simpson or Principal Skinner?

17. Mrs Krabappel, Marge Simpson or Maude Flanders places an ad in the lonely hearts column which Bart answers?

18. Soul singer Barry White once guest-starred in an episode of *The Simpsons*: true or false?

19. Homer wears an apron, a basketball vest or a bikini at a NASA press conference?

20. Who is struck by lightning to allow Lisa to win the local beauty pageant: Amber Dempsey, Allison Taylor or Maude Flanders?

21. Mr X reveals that Apu is selling what item as bagels?

22. The many layers of paint protected the Simpsons' house from a nuclear attack in a *Treehouse of Horror* episode: true or false?

23. Which restaurant tries to sue Homer after he eats almost everything on an "all you can eat" night: The Happy Sumo, The Rusty Barnacle or The Frying Dutchman?

24. Which character in the show wears bones in his hair: Sideshow Mel, the Comic Book Guy or Sideshow Bob?

25. Which police officer has a son called Ralph?

26. Detective Don Brodka works at what discount store: Try-N-Save, Kwik-E-Mart or Save-U-Shop?

27. After going back in time and killing a mosquito, Homer returns to the present to find which Springfield resident rules the world: Otto, Smithers, Ned Flanders or Reverend Lovejoy?

28. Who gets both of their arms stuck in a pair of vending machines and cannot go to the ballet as a result?

29. Mr Burns and some German businessmen eat at The Frying Dutchman, The Hungry Hun, The Berlin Buffet or The Munich Munch-U-Like restaurant?

30. What happens to Homer after he gets Bart to fill in his sanity test?

31. Bart reverses the charges to a telephone call to a schoolboy called Bruno Drundridge in which country: Australia, England, Switzerland or Albania?

32. Who does Marge, when she's a police officer, arrest for parking over three handicapped parking spaces?

33. Which member of the Beatles did Homer meet whilst he was a member of the Be Sharps?

34. After displaying Kim Basinger's underwear in his museum, Homer is forbidden to be within how many miles of any celebrity: 5, 50 or 500?

35. Who sells Bart's soul to the comic book dealer: Sideshow Bob, Krusty or Milhouse?

36. Who is the founder of the Pretzel Wagon franchise: Frank Ormand, Hans Moleman, Firehouse Ned or Professor Frink?

37. Nelson and Ralph were members of the boy band, the Party Posse: true or false?

38. For what publication does Homer become a restaurant critic?

39. Hank Scorpio is the president of which company: Kwik-E-Mart, the Krusty-O Cereal Corporation or the Globex Corporation?

40. Which famous pop star holds a private Valentine's Day concert for Apu and Manjula: Tom Jones, Robbie Williams, George Michael or Elton John?

41. What does Homer try to train Duncan the horse to do first: make him doughnuts, kick American footballs, pull a sledge or play ice hockey?

42. In what year does Marge say she and Homer met: 1966, 1969, 1971 or 1974?

43. Which member of the Simpson family wins the Springfield Art Fair with a portrait of a famous pop star?

44. Homer is prescribed marijuana by Dr Hibbert, Dr Riviera or Dr Putz?

45. Tipsy McStagger's is a drunken ex-newsreader, a cocktail at Moe's Tavern or a restaurant chain?

46. Who is sentenced to thirty days in jail after forgetting to pay for a bottle of bourbon: Marge, Homer or Barney?

47. When Bart is bullied by Nelson, who suggests he should fight dirty?

48. What is the name of the exhibition of ancient treasures Homer and Lisa break into the Springsonian Museum to see?

49. What is the name of Springfield's traffic reporter from the air: Professor Frink, Stephanie, Kent Brockman or Arnie Pie?

50. Bart buys a collie dog using a fake credit card but what is the name of the dog: Santa's Little Helper, Fang, Laddie or Pooch?

1. Who turns out to be the true leader of the Stonecutters: Homer, Maggie, Barney or Ned Flanders?

2. What is the name of the owner of the Military Antiques store in Springfield: Herman, Otto, Vincent or Jimbo?

3. The Ultimate Behemoth comes complete with four deep fat friers and its own satellite: true or false?

4. The loser of Homer and Ned's bet over mini-golf has to mow the other's lawn whilst wearing what item of clothing?

5. After Bart burns all the family's presents by mistake, does he: confess all, bury the presents and say burglars struck or go out to a shop and buy new ones with Homer's credit card?

6. Skateboarder Tony Hawk and which band appear in *The Simpsons* 300th episode: Blink 182, Level 42, E17 or Sham 69?

7. Which famous band joins the Simpsons at Moe's for a Thanksgiving dinner: U2, REM, *Nsync or M People?

8. Bart offends officials with a comedy routine when what event is soon to be staged in Springfield: the Superbowl, the Olympics, a *Jerry Springer* TV special or a WWF wrestling contest?

9. Who loses his TV show to Arthur Crandall and his dummy?

10. Bart uses whose telescope to spot what he thinks is a murder plot involving the Flanders family?

11. What name does Apu change the Kwik-E-Mart to after charging people to see Jasper frozen in the ice cream mart: The Ice Museum, Freak-E-Mart or Apu's Abnormal World?

12. Who buys Marge a bowling ball engraved with her name for her birthday?

13. MacArthur Parker is the show biz agent for Troy McClure, Milhouse or Mr Burns?

14. Where does Homer take on a second job to help pay for a present for Lisa: Kwik-E-Mart, Moe's Tavern or the Springfield Museum?

15. Captain McCallister is the owner of which Netherlands-based restaurant in Springfield?

16. Sir Putt-A-Lots is the site of a mini-golf tournament in which Bart takes part: true or false?

17. In the episode where Grampa gives his family their inheritance money, what is the name of the doll that Lisa buys: Malibu Stacy, Hollywood Heidi, California Hannah or Florida Pearl?

18. Who was about to sell Stampy the elephant to an ivory dealer before Stampy saves his life?

19. Which Springfield resident is unveiled as having a secret swimming pool on an Internet website: Mayor Quimby, Herman, Otto or Homer?

20. Who builds robots that turn on Mr Burns?

21. Which character, beginning with the letter D, has a belt that holds 8 cans of beer, a red cape and appears with two cheerleaders?

22. Who is the original coach of Bart's American Football team before Homer takes over: Ned Flanders, Principal Skinner or Chief Wiggum?

23. What is the name of the first ever cartoon featuring Itchy and Scratchy?

24. Who tries to disguise himself at a Springfield town meeting as Mr Snrub?

25. What breed of dog is Santa's Little Helper: a wolfhound, a greyhound or a bloodhound?

26. Security guard, Don Brodka, has a tattoo, a ponytail or an eyepatch?

27. What is the name of the lunchlady Lisa suspects of killing and cooking children in a *Treehouse of Horror* episode: Dana, Diane, Doris or Daisy?

28. Who does Bart believe Fat Tony has had murdered: Sideshow Bob, Reverend Lovejoy or Principal Skinner?

29. Who turns out to be a ballet natural but wears a ski mask to hide their identity?

30. Jericho operates a crime ring trading in fake diamonds, fake designer jeans, real diamonds or live elephants?

31. What product do the Frenchmen Ugolin and Cesar make: wine, cheese, doughnuts or cakes?

32. Homer and the University nerds try to steal what animal mascot of a rival institution?

33. Who starts the Museum of Hollywood Jerks in a camper van?

34. Who buys Bart's soul back for him from the comic book dealer: Homer, Milhouse or Lisa?

35. Which shady character does Homer turn to in order to get help for Marge's pretzel business: Professor Frink, Hans Moleman or Fat Tony?

36. The Party Posse's debut single contains hidden messages from which organization: the US Navy, the Russian KGB spy organization or the Girl Guides?

37. Springfield's restaurant owners try to kill Homer with a poisoned éclair, a poisoned shrimp or a poisoned burger?

38. Which member of the Simpsons is allergic to all the plant life in their new home at Cypress Creek?

39. Homer and some other men of Springfield lock Elton John in a dog carrier, an extra-large suitcase or a changing room locker?

40. Which character pays a thousand dollars for a hair growth product called Dimoxinil?

41. Who is killed at the opening day of a new auto-racing track: Sideshow Mel, Maude Flanders, Sideshow Bob or Rod Flanders?

42. Homer has a half brother; is his name Artie Ziff, Hans Moleman or Herb Powell?

43. Which two aliens threaten to destroy Earth until they read Maggie's mind?

44. Bono appeared as one of the singers on the 'Sending Our Love Down the Well' charity single: true or false?

45. Who cannot resist making shadow puppets when the optician switches off the lights: Lisa, Bart or Homer?

46. Homer knocks over the ancient Orb of Isis revealing that it is actually: a music box, a cigarette lighter or made in 1990?

47. Krusty is arrested for a robbery but which character actually committed the crime?

48. Is Bart skateboarding, walking, bicycling or scootering when he is knocked down by Mr Burns' car?

49. Who narrowly loses to Martin Prince for the class presidency: Bart, Milhouse or Nelson?

50. In *The Old Man and The Lisa* episode, who does a poor Mr Burns move in with?

★ ★   **QUIZ 17**   ★ ★

1. Which member of the family's photos is missing from the Simpson family album but is found stuck up at Homer's workplace?

2. Who provides video evidence that Homer did not mean to grab the bottom of Ashley Grant: Principal Skinner, Groundskeeper Willie or Maude Flanders?

3. Which one of Marge's sisters once had a relationship with Principal Skinner?

4. Who used Nacho Cheez as hair gel, drives a car called Li'l Bandit and has a long tattoo on his right arm?

5. Name one of the members of the Springfield Mensa group.

6. Who marries Homer's second wife in the episode called, *Brawl in The Family*?

7. Which member of the Simpson family was part of the group, the Be Sharps?

8. Which Springfield TV personality wins the lottery and starts wearing a gold medallion: Kent Brockman, Artie Ziff or Krusty the Clown?

9. Dolph and Kearney hang out with: Nelson, Jimbo Jones or Barney?

10. What item do Marge and Homer win at a dance competition at Greaser's Café: a motorbike, a deep fat-fryer or a years supply of hair gel?

11. Homer succeeds at the audition to do the voice of which cartoon character: Itchy, Radioactive Man or Poochie?

12. What sort of vehicle does Mindy Simmons drive or ride: a skateboard, a helicopter or a motorbike?

13. Are Marge's twin sisters older or younger than her?

14. In an episode in series 14, who proposes marriage to Edna Krabappel: Principal Skinner, Grampa Simpson or Mr Burns?

15. Which old rock 'n' roll star hosts the Teacher of the Year award: Elvis Presley, Fats Domino or Little Richard?

16. Who is voted King of the Mardi Gras in Springfield: Homer, Ned or Jimbo Jones?

17. What device takes old, unwanted letters and turns it into hamburger patty?

18. Which Springfield resident opened the Leftorium store: Ned, Moe, Barney or Mayor Quimby?

19. Sherri and Terri are twins in Bart's class, Lisa's class or in Marge's bridge club?

20. Who opens the Springfield Casino: Barney, Homer and Grampa or Mr Burns?

21. How many movie theatres does Springfield have: one, two, three or four?

22. When Lisa had a pony, did she call it: Princess, Brown Beauty, Bess or Queenie?

23. Who has a dog with the name, Crippler: Mayor Quimby, Mr Burns or Fat Tony?

24. The student from Albania who turned out to be a spy had a codename. Was it: Hawk, Budgie, Sparrow or Parrot?

25. Who nominates Mrs Krabappel for the Teacher of the Year award?

26. Who ran over Snowball I: Clovis Quimby, Mrs Krabappel or Chief Wiggum?

27. In *The Great Louse Detective* episode, what museum does Homer's float career towards: The History of Springfield, The Museum of Swordfish or The Dinosaurium?

28. Which schoolchild has an IQ of 216: Martin Prince, Bart or Lisa?

29. What 'insect' character is the star of the TV channel, Channel Ocho: Bumblebee Man, Cockroach Boy or Wasp Girl?

30. Was Ned Flanders a pharmacist, teacher or priest before he opened his store?

31. What name is sprayed as graffiti all over Springfield: Nelson, Ralph, El Barto or Freddy?

32. What was the 'sick' title of Barney's film entered in the Springfield Film Festival?

33. Which Springfield father turns out to be a lot older than he looks?

34. Which family live in a house with the house number, 742: the Simpsons, the Flanders or the Van Houtens?

35. Bart sold his soul to the devil but how many dollars did he get in return: one, five, 1,000, 5,000 or 100,000?

36. When Homer sold his soul in a different episode, what did he get in return: a new TV set, a doughnut, a new wife or $1 million?

37. Marge sometimes keeps the family savings in her hair: true or false?

38. Homer's mother left him a mural and: a poncho, an umbrella or a pair of boots?

39. Homer teaches 'How to have a successful marriage' at an Adult Education Centre: true or false?

40. Is Homer's favourite doughnut flavour: raspberry, strawberry or vanilla?

41. The Googolplex is one of Springfield's movie theatres. Can you name the other one?

42. Marge and Homer first met in detention at school, in a bowling alley or at Kamp Krusty?

43. Lisa's middle name is Emily: true or false?

44. Which TV superhero has the catchphrase, "Up and At 'Em": McBain, Krusty or Radioactive Man?

45. Which famous real-life computer businessman put Homer's Internet company out of business?

46. What is the door number of Patty and Selma's house: 199, 599, 1599 or 15911?

47. Mrs Pommelhorse teaches what subject at school: gymnastics, domestic science or biology?

48. Which famous actor took over the Kwik-E-Mart after Apu got fired: George Clooney, Kevin Kline or James Woods?

49. Which one of the following is Lisa's best friend in class: Alex Whitney, Jim Munson, Vicky Brooker or Janey Hagstrom?

50. In the opening credits, does the picture which hangs above the Simpsons' sofa usually show a ship, a burger, a mountain or a beach?

LISA
Level Questions

1. Yiddles is a store that sells magic tricks, practical jokes, medical supplies or all three?

2. What was the previous name of the dog called Santa's Little Helper?

3. Which one of these dogs did Santa's Little Helper not race against: Fido, Dog O' War, Rex or Chew My Shoe?

4. Who is the owner of Canine College to which the Simpsons' dog is sent?

5. The children of Springfield start the pirate radio show, "We Know All Your Secrets", after watching which creepy movie?

6. What does Homer order at the Itchy & Scratchy Land restaurant?

7. What is the name of the old couple who are neighbours of the Simpsons?

8. Which Springfield character drives a Hyundai car and has a son who he keeps in a drawer?

9. What is the first name of Chief Wiggum's wife?

10. What is the name of the co-worker Homer is attracted to and attends a convention with at Capital City?

11. Which inhabitant of Grampa Simpson's rest home turns out to be a successful cat burglar?

12. Sophie turns out to be the lost daughter of which Springfield character?

13. Homer pledges $10,000 to save his favourite British comedy show but what is it called?

14. What is the name of the health spa in which Homer is nearly killed in a steam room?

15. Homer is bet $50 by Bart that he cannot eat a whole box of which cooking ingredient?

16. Which doctor cures Ned Flanders after he checks in to a mental institution?

17. What nasty end occurs to Shary Bobbins as she floats away on her umbrella?

18. What is the name of the woman that Homer meets, who does the voices of Itchy and Scratchy?

19. When Moe turns his bar into a restaurant what name does he give it?

20. What is the name of the shopping mall built on Sabertooth Meadow?

21. Which father and son took over the Simpsons' house and changed the locks?

22. Santa's Little Helper mates with a greyhound and has how many puppies?

23. In the second *Who Shot Mr Burns* episode, who is the second person to go into police custody?

24. Lisa joins up with an environmental group led by a teenager she has a crush on. What is his name?

25. On the Internet, Homer calls himself by what mystery name?

26. When Lisa has a date with Nelson, in which unlikely building do they kiss?

27. What is the name of the doll that Lisa gets doll designer, Stacy Lovell, to design?

28. After release from prison, Sideshow Bob supervises the building of what object?

29. What is the name of the military academy Bart is enrolled in after deafening the people of Springfield using megaphones?

30. Larry Kittkill is the owner of which place in Springfield?

31. Can you name one of the leaders of the real Hell's Satans motorcycle gang?

32. Which founding member of the brainy Superfriends has black hair and red glasses?

33. In *Lard of the Dance*, what is the name of the new student Lisa shows around school?

34. In *Treehouse of Horror IX*, what TV show do the Simpsons and aliens appear on to settle custody of Maggie?

35. Homer reads an overdue library book of classic tales that include Lisa as which historical figure?

36. Homer is prescribed marijuana after his eyes are injured by an attack from what creatures?

37. Marge helps a prisoner called Jack who has a talent for what subject?

38. In the *This Little Wiggy* episode, Bart and Ralph visit a toy store where there is a giant fairground ferris wheel. What is the name of the store?

39. Who was Springfield's Sanitation Commissioner before Homer won the post in an election?

40. Brad and Neil are executives for what brand of nutrition bar?

41. Lisa's scientific tests prove that which creature is smarter than Bart?

42. When Homer goes to Springfield University, which of the nerds that he meets wears a calculator on his hip?

43. Where does Bart find Mr Burns' lost teddy bear?

44. What is the name of the airport bar that Homer is in when he's mistaken for a pilot?

45. Which fellow vegetarians does Apu introduce Lisa to on the roof of the Kwik-E-Mart?

46. How heavy does Homer have to become before he is declared disabled and allowed to work at home?

47. How many pairs of swimming trunks does Martin Prince turn up to the Simpsons' new pool wearing?

48. What is the name of the only child of Reverend Lovejoy and his wife?

49. What is Homer's final act when he is having a debate with Artie Ziff?

50. Whose bottom does Homer spot a piece of candy stuck to which he grabs, sparking news stories and demonstrations?

★ ★ ★　　　QUIZ 2　　　★ ★ ★

1. Which real-life boy band does Bart's boy band get tips from?

2. The Simpsons win an African safari where they are chased by a hippo but saved by what sort of creature?

3. Bart is placed on an experimental drug to improve his attention deficit disorder. What is the drug called?

4. Which phone company make a deal with Homer to place a massive phone tower on the Simpsons' house roof?

5. What is the name of the judge who sentences Bart and Homer to be tied together after Bart steals Chief Wiggum's police car?

6. Which much-loved multi-millionaire opens a store in Springfield making Mr Burns wish he was loved as well?

7. What bowling score does Homer obtain becoming a local celebrity as a result?

8. In *Treehouse of Horror XII*, what does Marge grow?

9. What do Lisa and Homer go to after spending time in sensory deprivation tanks?

10. Bart answers a lonely hearts entry placed by his schoolteacher but with what name?

11. Which famous short movie actor provided the voice of Homer's brother?

12. Which congressman does Lisa catch accepting a bribe to drill for oil in a statue's head?

13. Who gives Homer a sanity test after he's found at work wearing a pink shirt?

14. What is the stage name of Shawna Tifton when she dances?

15. What is the name of the owner of the Kids First Industry which takes over the running of Bart and Lisa's school?

16. Which boy band creator rescues Bart from a mob after Bart cheated in the Springfield marathon?

17. What does Homer paper-fold a one million yen banknote into before it gets blown away?

18. The first Simpsons vacation seen in the show was to which canyon?

19. In the *Worst Episode Ever*, who does the Comic Book Guy fall in love with?

20. What sort of wild animals does Marge round up using her Canyonero vehicle, saving her family?

21. What is the full name of the founder of the town of Springfield?

22. What is the name of the satellite which comes free with the Ultimate Behemoth camper vehicle?

23. Whilst piloting a boat in Florida, Homer runs over a celebrity alligator known by what name?

24. Who is Bart and Lisa's Sunday School teacher?

25. What planet are the aliens Kodos and Kang from?

26. Moe appears in a Duff Beer calendar, but what happens to his face in the calendar?

27. What was Bart's character when he acted in adverts as a baby?

28. Why does Homer take off his wedding ring which makes two women think he is single?

29. When Homer decides to become a hippie, can you name one of the two hippie friends of his mother's he becomes friends with?

30. How much was the reverse charges phone call Bart made to Australia which causes a diplomatic incident?

31. Who is the Undersecretary of State for International Protocol: Brat and Punk Division?

32. Who is to kick Bart in the butt as part of Bart's apology to the Australian people?

33. What word did Bart try to get tattooed on himself in the first full-length episode of *The Simpsons*?

34. What is the slogan of Costington's store?

35. Ned and Homer are beaten up in Las Vegas by many people including the Moody Blues: true or false?

36. Which tramp claims to have invented the Itchy character in *Itchy & Scratchy* cartoons?

37. What is the name of the two children, who look very much like Lisa and Bart, who prove the US Postal service stole a cartoon from the owner of Itchy & Scratchy studios?

38. In *Treehouse of Horror VII*, what is the name of Bart's evil twin brother?

39. Where do Lisa and Bart find some plutonium when searching for batteries for the TV remote control?

40. When Homer moans to Marge in an episode about no one respecting him, what does Bart write on the back of his head?

41. When the Simpsons become farmers, what two crops does Homer cross?

42. What is the name of the director of Springfield Theatrical Productions?

43. Gloria's old boyfriend, Snake, kidnaps her and Homer. Who was her new boyfriend at the time?

44. Dr Marvin Monroe's Family Therapy Centre offers family bliss or what back?

45. In *The Simpsons 138th Episode Spectacular*, who is shown as a bald, one-eyed man?

46. What computer game is Bart caught shoplifting by security guard, Don Brodka?

47. What cash prize does Bart turn down to choose the alternative prize of a real elephant?

48. What household item have the Simpsons been saving up to buy only to spend the money twice on a saxophone for Lisa?

49. Homer volunteers Bart for a young American Football team. What is its name?

50. When standing together in their Springfield Wildcats uniform, what number is made by the religious Todd and Rod Flanders?

Recent episodes

1. In *Mommie Beerest*, does the health inspector die eating one of Moe's: burgers, pickled eggs or corndogs?

2. In *All's Fair in Oven War*, which member of the Simpsons family entered the Ovenfresh Bakeoff?

3. Does Nelson, Bart, Barney or Homer work with Goose Gladwell to become a t-shirt mogul?

4. In *The Bart of War* episode, Bart and Milhouse stumble across a massive collection of Beatles memorabilia at whose house?

5. Was Jim Proudfoot a member of the Sioux, Pawnee or Mohican native American tribe?

6. What giant piece of office equipment attacks soldiers at the start of *The Heartbroke Kid*?

7. In *Fraudcast News*, who climbs up Geezer Rock and pulls out a tree, only to cause the entire rock to collapse?

8. In *Bart-Mangled Banner*, what pet was each of the three Simpson children given just before going to the doctors?

9. Which children's TV character was one of the prisoners at the Ronald Reagan Re-education Centre along with Bill Clinton and The Simpsons: Elmo, Itchy, Snoopy or the Cookie Monster?

10. Which of Homer's friends had a bit part in the horror film, *The Re-Deadening*: Lenny, Carl or Barney?

11. In *The Way We Weren't*, who was the subject of Milhouse's first ever kiss?

12. Which famous religious figure does the Pie Man refuse to hit with a pie?

13. Which English King was Homer portrayed as when marrying actress Jane Seymour in the *Margical History Tour* episode?

14. Who sleeps on a giant tongue at the Springfield Natural History Museum?

15. What animal tears off Bart's shorts, making him bare his bottom at the American flag?

16. In *The Bart of War*, what item of gym equipment does Homer dump in the river?

17. Who had been hiding in the Simpsons' attic, living off water he could suck off the house's rafters: Mr Burns, Chief Wiggum or Artie Ziff?

18. Who drinks cocktails from his fridge made of Slimfast diet drink and champagne?

19. As which classical composer is Bart portrayed in the episode, *Margical History Tour*?

20. Whose Bar Mitzvah is televised and features The Beach Boys Experience and Mr T?

21. Who is Springfield superhero, Pie Man?

22. In *Don't Fear The Roofer*, what is the name of Homer's imaginary friend who turns out to be real: Ray, Herb or Leonardo?

23. In *Future-Drama*, who does Professor Frink predict will be Lisa's prom date: Hans Moleman, Nelson Muntz or Milhouse?

24. Ravencrow Neversmiles is the new Goth name of which Simpsons character after an image change?

25. Who taught Bart from the book Math Safari after Lisa took out a restraining order on her brother?

26. At which big store does Grandpa become a store greeter before he crashes into a display of garden gnomes: Conningtons, Sprawlmart or Coolworths?

27. In *Co-Dependents Day*, Homer and Marge become addicted to drinking after visiting Moe's Tavern, the Lush Valley Winery or the Duff Brewery?

28. In *The Way We Weren't*, how old was Homer when he had his first ever kiss?

29. In *On A Clear Day I Can't See My Sister*, what do Bart, Lisa and the other kids have to be at school for 3am to go on a field trip to see?

30. Howell Huser gives Springfield what mark out of ten causing the town's businesses to close down?

31. In *Pranksta Rap*, which famous rapper offers Bart a place on his world tour: 50 Cent, Snoop Doggy Dogg or Ice-T?

32. In *My Big Fat Greek Wedding*, which teacher has a party featuring Duffman before her marriage to Principal Skinner?

33. When Bart and Lisa return Homer's motorhome to Bob's RV Round-Up, what giant inflatable creature floats above the motorhome dealers?

34. In *The Seven Beer Snitch*, what rival town mocks Springfield?

35. In *Sleeping With The Enemy*, whose teeth does Homer use as a beer bottle opener?

36. Whose t-shirt business includes t-shirts featuring characters Scratchbob Itchpants and Osami Bin Scratchy?

37. Who is forced to sing '99 Red Balloons' to entertain German youth hostellers to earn a tip?

38. Who is buried underneath the collapsing Geezer Rock in *Fraudcast News*?

39. Who is taken to a maximum security fat camp where one of the inmates is newsreader Kent Brockman?

40. Who won ownership of the Ziffcorp company in a poker game?

41. In *Future-Drama*, who turns out to be dating Marge eight years into the future?

42. Whose badge reads 'cash bribes only' when catching Bart planning a fake wedding?

43. As a child, why did Homer have to wear an eyepatch whilst at summer camp: he injured himself with a switchblade, a fizzy drinks bottle or hot jam from a donut?

44. Which member of the Simpson household turns out to have an IQ of 167 in *Smart and Smarter*?

45. In *Don't Fear The Roofer*, which famous scientist is one of the guests at Lenny's party held in Moe's Tavern?

46. In *There's Something About Marrying*, what job does the person do who is planning to marry Marge's sister, Patty?

47. Which Springfield character introduces himself as Jeff Albertson to Ned Flanders when Homer does a dance with the inflatable octopus: Nelson Muntz, Comic Book Guy or The Mysterious Stranger?

48. What is the name of the newspaper that Lisa starts to publish in *Fraudcast News*?

49. Does Mayor Quimby, William Shatner, Mr Burns or Fred Gehry turn the Springfield concert hall into a new prison?

50. What magazine does Homer read in his hammock when Bart asks for 50 dollars to go to see the Murder for Life rap concert?

1. In *She Used To Be My Girl*, Chloe used to date Barney, Grandpa or Apu before she left Springfield to become a news reporter?

2. Who sells his dances to an American Football player after his dancing becomes a phenomenon on the internet?

3. In *Sleeping with the Enemy*, who does Nelson's Mum start to date: Moe, Barney or Carl?

4. In *Treehouse of Horror XV*, which member of the Simpsons family kept eating themselves inside the alien's oven?

5. What sort of transport device does Inspector Wiggum try to escape from Victorian London in?

6. What giant food item lures the hoard of Homer clones into a deep canyon?

7. Which Springfield character is turned into a half cow who Homer has to milk?

8. Who does Bart sell his skateboard to in order to buy snacks from the new school vending machines?

9. Tab Spangle is head of the Serenity Ranch, the Kwik-E-Mart or Disco Stu Records Inc?

10. Who entered a crayon sandwich in the Overfresh bake-off competition: Lisa, Ralph, Nelson or Milhouse?

11. Who steals plutonium from the Springfield nuclear power plant to help Lisa's science fair project?

12. When the Simpsons travel to China to help Selma get a baby, what toy do three foreign invaders use to try to scale the Great Wall of China?

13. Who runs the Strip for your Wife course that Homer attends?

14. Is the name of the girl who escapes the juvenile prison handcuffed to Bart: Gina, Tania or Sonia?

15. What nationality were the coach tourists who came to see Homer after his dance had been beamed round the world via the internet?

16. What endangered species of animal does Homer first try to smuggle out of China and then try to strangle?

17. Who announced on TV that Marge Simpson had won an Oops Patrol t-shirt?

18. Who resigns as school president and calls a strike of all the students in protest of art, music and gym classes being cancelled?

19. What is the name of the young children's TV star who Maggie becomes addicted to and Marge gets tickets to see?

20. What body feature do all the Homer clones in *Treehouse of Horror* lack: a belly button, body hair or nipples?

21. Does Lenny, Moe, Marge or Carl buy Homer a DVD player and the first season of Magnum PI for Christmas?

22. What type of giant sweet does Homer take a bite out of whilst shrunk in size and in Mr Burn's stomach?

23. Which old arcade game characters got married in the half-time show on Superbowl 16?

24. In *Catch Em If You Can*, who flies to Miami instead of visiting Uncle Tyrone?

25. In *Treehouse of Horror XIII*, who comes back from the dead at a seance to introduce the horrific tales?

26. How much wine did Marge drink before she fought with her old schoolfriend Chloe Talbot on their lawn: half a glass, three glasses or six glasses?

27. How much did the Simpson's new kitchen cost: US$10,000, US$50,000, US$100,000 or US$250,000?

28. Who accidentally swallows Maggie in a shrunken capsule containing a lifetime's supply of vitamins?

29. What is the name of the female Global News Network reporter who comes to Springfield to cover a scandal involving Mayor Quimby?

30. Lisa named the replacement for Snowball II after a jazz musician. Was its name: Coltrane, Miles Davies or Duke Ellington?

31. Who has to pretend to be Selma's husband so that she can adopt a baby from China?

32. Can you name both of the children who carried Peruvian fighting frogs in boxes for show and tell in class?

33. Who appeared to build a robot when in fact they were inside the machine moving it around?

34. Whose father ate a chocolate bar, had a terrible peanut allergy and was captured by a circus only to be rescued by Bart?

35. What animal in a box does Nelson give the twins at school to make them smell and stop them abusing Lisa?

36. In *C.E. Doh*, does Mr Burns say he worked at the power plant for 22, 42 or 62 years?

37. In *Treehouse of Horror XV*, which two of the Simpsons were baked in pies inside the alien's oven?

38. Whose biblical films does Mr Burns invest in only for Marge to walk out of the screening?

39. When Madam Wu asks Homer what his job is, does he say: nuclear power plant worker, Chinese acrobat, brain surgeon or hired hit man?

40. At the funeral of Snowball II, was the name of Marge's guinea pig she lost as a child: Rosemary, Cinnamon or Saffron?

41. Who leaves his flatmates Julio and Grady to go to Medieval Times theme restaurant: Ned, Cletus, Artie Ziff or Homer?

42. Who rented out his house to college students to get the money to buy everyone in Springfield a Christmas present?

43. When Marge's hair started to burn after she rescued Lisa from the lava, how long does Marge say it will take for the fire to reach her head: ten minutes, an hour, two hours or a week?

44. What item of garden furniture keeps cloning Homers in a *Treehouse of Horror* episode?

45. In *The President Wore Pearls*, what number did Homer put all his money on and thought he won US$200,000: 7, 17, 27 or 37?

46. Who was driving Selma when she had a hot flush, was thrown from the car and melted a hole in the snow?

47. What is the name of the bookstore in which Marge hears Esme Delacroix give a reading?

48. Which foreign city refuses to be Springfield's sister city after all the toddlers went on the rampage at a children's TV show concert?

49. Who swooped down in a helicopter to save Chloe Talbot just moments before red hot lava would have killed her?

50. What is the name of the book Marge wrote which gets the whole of Springfield gossiping?

HOMER
Level Answers

1. Maggie
2. Marge
3. Bart
4. Springfield
5. Three
6. Homer
7. Springfield Elementary
8. Beer
9. A teacher
10. Bart

11. Little hair
12. Otto
13. Mr Burns
14. Two
15. Loathe Homer
16. Blue
17. "D'oh!"
18. Kwik-E-Mart
19. Krusty
20. Quimby

21. Mr Burns
22. False
23. The living room
24. Selma
25. Yellow
26. True

27. Principal of Springfield Elementary School
28. Patty
29. Maude Flanders
30. Bart

31. Ned Flanders
32. Saxophone
33. Shelbyville
34. Two
35. Wendell
36. Lovejoy
37. Ned Flanders
38. Yes
39. TV newsreader
40. *Treehouse of Horror*

41. A tie
42. Three
43. Moe's Tavern
44. Friends of Bart's
45. Principal Skinner
46. Bart
47. The sofa
48. Maggie
49. 'Do the Bartman'
50. Bart

QUIZ 2

1. Lisa
2. Saxophone
3. Bart
4. Abe

5. True
6. False
7. Friend
8. Grampa Simpson

9. Flanders
10. Doughnuts

11. Moe
12. Excellent
13. Snowball
14. Bart
15. A dog
16. James Brown
17. False
18. Bart
19. True
20. A fish

21. Dr Hibbert
22. Lisa
23. True
24. Nelson
25. True
26. True
27. Yellow
28. Homer
29. Todd Flanders

30. Ned Flanders

31. False
32. Homer's dad
33. A nuclear power plant
34. Otto
35. India
36. Ralph Wiggum
37. Milhouse
38. Ned Flanders'
39. The same school
40. Otto

41. Bart
42. False
43. By bicycle
44. Duff's
45. Homer
46. Blue #56
47. Ringo Starr
48. Moe's Tavern
49. Scottish
50. Green

MARGE
Level Answers

1. History test
2. Ping-pong
3. Martin Prince
4. Herman
5. Baseball
6. The Simpsons
7. The Olympics
8. Ned Flanders
9. The church
10. The Springfield Gorge

11. Homer
12. Nude-E-Mart
13. The founder of Springfield
14. Bumtown
15. Falafels
16. Pinchy
17. Homer
18. Barney
19. $1 million
20. A church

21. The Magic Palace
22. Samantha Stanky
23. Krusty the Clown
24. Limited to three handguns or less
25. Bart

26. True
27. Bart
28. True
29. Princess Kashmir
30. Michael Jackson

31. Patty and Selma
32. Bouys
33. Terror Lake
34. J (Homer J Simpson)
35. Milhouse's
36. Bart's
37. Springfield Isotopes
38. Xena, Warrior Princess
39. The Denver Broncos
40. A funeral procession

41. The Lucky Savage
42. Homecoming Queen
43. Bart
44. True
45. False
46. Lisa
47. A camper van
48. A windmill
49. *Mom Monthly*
50. Mr Burns

1. Divorced
2. "Eat My Shorts"
3. Herman
4. Homer

5. Ralph Wiggum
6. Less than $25
7. Thanksgiving
8. A ventriloquist doll

9. Bart
10. Jacques

11. Lisa
12. Moe's Tavern
13. Martin Prince
14. Bowling
15. A burger
16. Grampa Simpson
17. Beer
18. Sanjay
19. Mouldy Maggie
20. Stampy

21. A country and western singer
22. His half-brother
23. Mr Black
24. King Homer
25. Barney
26. Principal Skinner
27. Nachos Rifles Alcohol
28. Scratchy

29. Leonard Nimoy (Spock)
30. Homer

31. $13
32. A tattoo
33. Smithers
34. Snowball II
35. Homer
36. Sideshow Bob
37. False
38. Albania
39. Homer's
40. Red

41. True
42. The family quilt
43. Bart
44. Yes
45. Stephen Hawking
46. Chief Wiggum
47. Marge
48. Bart
49. Kwik-E-Mart
50. A giant catfish

★ ★ QUIZ 3 ★ ★

1. The Babysitter Bandit
2. 908
3. Groundskeeper Willie
4. Monopoly
5. At a Las Vegas casino
6. Snake
7. The Springfield Speedway
8. A cow's heart
9. Selma
10. Cold pet rat

11. Homer, Sideshow Mel, Ron Howard
12. True
13. Marge

14. A stapling gun
15. A gas explosion
16. Potato chips
17. A French circus
18. Dr Hibbert
19. France
20. Babysitter

21. First
22. Ned Flanders
23. *Taxicab Conversations*
24. The Holy Rollers
25. Marge
26. Reverend Lovejoy's
27. True

28. Bart
29. True
30. Homer

31. Chief Wiggum
32. A flower
33. The Flanders
34. Apu
35. Francine
36. Nelson
37. Lucius Sweet
38. True
39. True

40. Barney

41. Dr Hibbert
42. Discount Lion Safari
43. Mayor Quimby
44. The Space Shuttle
45. Guns
46. Bart and Lisa
47. The TV set
48. Mr Sparkle
49. A hot air balloon
50. Charlie

★ ★   QUIZ 4   ★ ★

1. D–
2. Knight Boat
3. Wiggum
4. Santa's Little Helper
5. As a mascot
6. True
7. Patty and Selma
8. In Las Vegas
9. A skateboard
10. Scratchy

11. *Space Mutants IV*
12. Eight
13. Marge's
14. "Aye carumba"
15. Homer
16. *The Simpsons*
17. Policeman
18. True
19. The Animotion
20. "Eat My Shorts"

21. Snowball I
22. Football
23. True
24. Buckingham Palace
25. George Bush

26. Black
27. U2
28. Lisa
29. Mr Burns
30. True

31. The Thompsons
32. Fruit juice
33. A whole roast suckling pig
34. False
35. Lisa
36. False
37. One
38. False
39. A phone book
40. Ned Flanders

41. Fat Tony
42. 1980
43. Lisa
44. Snakes
45. Pork Princess
46. A camper van
47. Mr Burns
48. Grampa Simpson
49. $847.63
50. True

★★ QUIZ 5 ★★

1. 600 days
2. Lisa
3. Batman
4. Barney
5. A cigar
6. Ned Flanders
7. A rock guitarist
8. Lisa
9. Milhouse
10. Stephanie

11. Kent Brockman
12. Make list
13. Eat doughnuts
14. Tell-off the boss
15. Ned Flanders
16. A crayon
17. Barney
18. Martin Sheen
19. Tom Jones
20. Krusty

21. Troy McClure
22. Dr Hibbert
23. False
24. Disco Stu
25. True
26. None

27. Ice hockey
28. Mr Burns
29. Bart's treehouse
30. Mr Burns

31. Cletus
32. Food jumps off people's plates
33. A lobster
34. Apu's
35. Giraffe
36. Larry
37. A biplane
38. Homer's
39. Florida
40. Bea Simmons

41. Broccoli
42. Li'l Lightning
43. Lisa
44. Russian
45. Karl
46. Muntz
47. Fidel Castro
48. Grease
49. The Happy Sumo
50. False

★★ QUIZ 6 ★★

1. Lucille
2. *Cheers*
3. The ring toss stall
4. Selma Bouvier
5. His chest
6. Stephen Hawking
7. Largest human pyramid

8. A barbershop quartet
9. *Itchy & Scratchy*
10. Sideshow Bob

11. True
12. A reindeer
13. Bart

14. Marge
15. Buzz Aldrin
16. True
17. Maggie
18. Packets of frozen foods
19. Bart
20. True

21. Christmas
22. Bart
23. Barney
24. Homer
25. Pennsylvania
26. Allison Taylor
27. Ice hockey
28. Agent Mulder
29. Ned Flanders
30. A jack-in-the-box

31. Lisa

32. Nelson Muntz
33. Spanky
34. Correct grammar
35. Mr Burns and Grampa
36. The Maison Derriere
37. Senor Ding-Dong
38. State Governor
39. Otto
40. A fez hat

41. A dolphin
42. Nelson's
43. Rancho Relaxo
44. Termites
45. Tom Jones
46. Water balloons
47. Cuba
48. Lisa
49. Blowfish
50. One

★ ★ QUIZ 7 ★ ★

1. A comet
2. Mr Burns
3. Ralph Wiggum
4. Hitler's car
5. Lindsey Naegle
6. "We're Now Rat-Free"
7. Kent Brockman
8. True
9. Bart
10. Cecil

11. Bart
12. Homer
13. Your Name on a Burger
14. A prison
15. True
16. Capital City
17. Itchy

18. False
19. Bouvier
20. Manjula

21. Apu
22. Barbara
23. Bobo
24. False
25. Germany
26. Homer
27. England
28. Wine
29. Thomas Edison
30. Grampa's

31. Lobster
32. Marge
33. Praise Land

34. Red
35. The Nazis
36. Three
37. Bleeding Gums Murphy
38. Marge Simpson
39. A dolphin
40. Brown

41. A monkey

42. 1895
43. Principal Skinner
44. Albert Einstein
45. Bleeding Gums Murphy
46. Homer
47. The Simpsons'
48. $500,000
49. Maude Flanders
50. Frank Grimes

★ ★ **QUIZ 8** ★ ★

1. Lisa
2. The Flanders'
3. Smithers
4. Marge
5. Bart
6. Roger Myers
7. Jub Jub
8. Princess Kashmir
9. Destroy them
10. John

11. His treehouse
12. A yo-yo
13. Spinal Tap
14. True
15. Homer
16. Amber Dempsey
17. Homer
18. Jimbo Jones
19. Ice cream van
20. Milhouse

21. A sponge
22. The Rolling Stones
23. Marge Simpson
24. A doughnut
25. Itchy & Scratchy International
26. Uter

27. False
28. A rare ancient statue
29. Daddy
30. The Rolling Stones

31. Jimbo Jones, Ned Flanders
32. An automated hammer
33. Homer
34. Homer
35. Kirk
36. Miracle Maude
37. Easter
38. A bear
39. Montgomery (Monty)
40. When the TV breaks down

41. Art
42. Because he has his broken jaw wired up
43. The Who
44. Grampa Simpson
45. Homer
46. The Comic Book Guy
47. Use electric shocks on each other
48. Channel 6
49. The Simpsons'
50. Principal Skinner

★ ★ QUIZ 9 ★ ★

1. A candy trade show
2. True
3. The school psychologist
4. Maggie
5. Maggie
6. Todd Flanders
7. Godzilla
8. Arthur Crandall
9. Groundskeeper Willie
10. Bart

11. Hawaii
12. A clown
13. Bart
14. A pony
15. Groundskeeper Willie
16. Pierce Brosnan
17. Apu's
18. A real-life African elephant
19. Tim Henman and Andre Agassi
20. A massage chair

21. New York
22. Bart
23. Mr Burns
24. A monorail
25. Fakes his own death

26. The Happy Sailor
27. Torture Land and Explosion Land
28. A bar tender
29. Ned Flanders
30. France

31. Nuclear physics
32. Marty
33. Says they will never see her family again
34. Kirk Van Houten
35. Basketball
36. Freddy
37. Homer
38. Ned Flanders
39. True
40. False

41. $1 million
42. A badger
43. Sideshow Bob
44. True
45. Helicopter blades
46. Sanitation Commissioner
47. True
48. Mr Burns
49. Lisa
50. Lisa

★ ★ QUIZ 10 ★ ★

1. Mrs Krabappel's
2. *Rock Bottom*
3. Krusty
4. Martin Prince
5. Fallout Boy
6. The Isotopes
7. Japan

8. His mouth
9. The Flanders'
10. False

11. The Rusty Barnacle
12. A bucket
13. Krusty the Clown

14. Bart
15. Shelbyville
16. Mr Burns
17. Lion tamers
18. False
19. Ned Flanders
20. Venus Williams

21. An airship
22. Widow's Peak
23. Marge
24. Mother Simpson
25. True
26. Ozzy Osbourne
27. Ruth Powers
28. True
29. Sheep
30. True

31. True
32. Sideshow Bob

33. A robin
34. Las Vegas
35. Bart
36. Out-of-date coleslaw
37. Tom Sawyer
38. Homer's
39. Milhouse
40. Artie Ziff

41. Homer's workplace
42. Artie Ziff
43. Krusty
44. Germany
45. Homer
46. False
47. Homer
48. Move the town five miles away
49. Senator Mendoza
50. Mel Gibson

★ ★ QUIZ 11 ★ ★

1. Venus de Milo
2. Head of the local mafia
3. Mr Burns
4. Department of Motor Vehicles
5. Lisa
6. The Emperor of Japan
7. True
8. The Singing Sirloin
9. Mrs Bouvier
10. Jay Leno

11. Gone Fission
12. A pirate
13. A pony
14. Homer
15. Ronan Keating
16. Krustyburger

17. Bill and Marty
18. Lisa
19. True
20. Kamp Krusty

21. New York
22. Bart
23. An iguana
24. Mother Simpson
25. Springfield Downs
26. A pony
27. A+
28. Itchy & Scratchy Land
29. Krusty the Clown
30. The Flanders

31. Bart
32. Lizards

33. *McBain*
34. Marge
35. Mr Burns
36. Lisa
37. Dolly Parton
38. True
39. Karl
40. The Pope

41. Greta
42. Down a well
43. A horse
44. George Bush
45. *Be-Bop Idol*
46. Rainer Wolfcastle
47. $100
48. Homer
49. Chief Wiggum
50. Sabertooth Meadow

★★ QUIZ 12 ★★

1. Mr Burns
2. Don Vittorio
3. Ralph Wiggum
4. Fish gutters
5. Homer
6. Green
7. Grampa
8. A new car
9. Bart
10. Britney Spears

11. Holliss Hurlbut
12. Barney
13. The Beer N' Brawl
14. Malibu Stacy dolls
15. Homer
16. False
17. Seven and eight
18. China
19. Tom Jones
20. Television

21. Sideshow Bob
22. Manjula
23. Snake
24. Maggie
25. A radio talk show host
26. Krusty the Clown

27. Made of metal
28. Red
29. Snake's
30. Milhouse

31. Homer
32. Smithers
33. Pyjamas, electric toothbrushes, cough syrup
34. The Superbowl
35. Nelson Muntz
36. Not So Crazy Horse
37. Grampa Simpson
38. Greta Wolfcastle
39. Horse stables
40. American Football

41. Slithers
42. Ugly teeth braces
43. Dr Hibbert
44. 48
45. The Murderhorn
46. Three
47. Dr Riviera
48. $100
49. Martin's
50. An angel

★★ QUIZ 13 ★★

1. Milhouse	27. Snowball
2. Labelled a child genius	28. Karate
3. False	29. A black cape
4. The airport	30. $500
5. Capital City	
6. A classmate of Bart's	31. Milhouse
7. Sideshow Mel	32. Sideshow Bob
8. Richard Nixon	33. A parasail
9. Homer	34. False
10. Renee	35. Mr Burns
	36. True
11. Barney	37. Homer
12. Jebediah Springfield	38. American Football
13. True	39. An art gallery
14. Brad Goodman	40. Mr Burns
15. "I didn't do it"	
16. Springfield policemen	41. Principal Skinner
17. False	42. Brazil
18. A panda	43. Red
19. Bart	44. Cashew nuts
20. Word-improving tapes	45. The mountain above Homer cracks and falls away
21. Grampa Simpson	46. Jimbo
22. 'Do the Bartman'	47. Captain Lance Murdock
23. Homer	48. Homer
24. Dr Riviera	49. The Mathemagician
25. Sideshow Bob	50. Homer
26. Sideshow Bob	

★★ QUIZ 14 ★★

1. Dr Zweig	9. Buddhism
2. The Stonecutters	10. Maude Flanders
3. Shelbyville	
4. Poor Violet	11. Allison Taylor
5. The Loch Ness Monster	12. Homer
6. His hammock	13. Only in males
7. Principal Skinner	14. Homer
8. Mr Burns	15. Martin Prince

16. They get fired
17. Barney
18. True
19. The Party Posse
20. Air force

21. Mr Burns
22. False
23. A daughter
24. Krusty
25. New York
26. Bleeding Gums Murphy
27. Ron Howard
28. Jay
29. Bart
30. Mother

31. Gravy
32. Mulder and Scully from
    The X Files

33. Duff Beer
34. A space satellite
35. Moe
36. Cypress Creek
37. Moe
38. Max Power
39. Bart
40. Mr Burns

41. Furious D
42. The janitor's cupboard
43. Googoplex
44. Homer
45. Karl and Lenny
46. A joke shop
47. *Casablanca*
48. Mr Teeny
49. $12 million
50. Red Blazer Realty

★★ QUIZ 15 ★★

1. Maggie
2. The Stonecutters
3. Santa's Little Helper
4. A fish
5. The Christmas tree
6. Venice
7. Mouthwash
8. M
9. Captain Lance Murdock
10. A swimming pool

11. Moe
12. Selma
13. April Flowers
14. *The Springfield Shopper*
15. Chief Wiggum
16. Mr Burns
17. Mrs Krabappel
18. True

19. An apron
20. Amber Dempsey

21. Week-old doughnuts
22. True
23. The Frying Dutchman
24. Sideshow Mel
25. Chief Wiggum
26. Try-N-Save
27. Ned Flanders
28. Homer
29. The Hungry Hun
30. He gets sent to a mental
    institution

31. Australia
32. Homer
33. George Harrison
34. 500 miles

35. Milhouse
36. Frank Ormand
37. True
38. *The Springfield Shopper*
39. Globex Corporation
40. Elton John

41. Kick American footballs
42. 1974

43. Marge
44. Dr Hibbert
45. A restaurant chain
46. Marge
47. Homer
48. Treasures of Isis
49. Arnie Pie
50. Laddie

★★   **QUIZ 16**   ★★

1. Homer
2. Herman
3. True
4. Their wife's best dress
5. Bury the presents and say burglars struck
6. Blink 182
7. REM
8. The Olympics
9. Krusty the Clown
10. Lisa's

11. Freak-E-Mart
12. Homer
13. Troy McClure
14. Kwik-E-Mart
15. The Frying Dutchman
16. True
17. Malibu Stacy
18. Homer
19. Mayor Quimby
20. Professor Frink

21. Duffman
22. Ned Flanders
23. *Steamboat Itchy*
24. Mr Burns
25. Greyhound

26. A tattoo
27. Doris
28. Principal Skinner
29. Bart
30. Fake designer jeans

31. Wine
32. A pig mascot
33. Homer
34. Lisa
35. Fat Tony
36. The US Navy
37. A poisoned éclair
38. Lisa
39. A dog carrier
40. Homer

41. Maude Flanders
42. Herb Powell
43. Kang and Kodos
44. False
45. Homer
46. A music box
47. Sideshow Bob
48. Skateboarding
49. Bart
50. Smithers

★ ★ QUIZ 17 ★ ★

1. Maggie
2. Groundskeeper Willie
3. Patty
4. Snake
5. Dr Hibbert, the Comic Book Guy, Lindsey Naegle, Professor Frink, Principal Skinner
6. Grampa Simpson
7. Homer
8. Kent Brockman
9. Jimbo Jones
10. A motorbike

11. Poochie
12. A motorbike
13. Older
14. Principal Skinner
15. Little Richard
16. Homer
17. The George Foreman Mail Sorter
18. Ned Flanders
19. Bart's class
20. Mr Burns

21. Two
22. Princess
23. Mr Burns

24. Sparrow
25. Bart
26. Clovis Quimby
27. The Museum of Swordfish
28. Martin Prince
29. Bumblebee Man
30. A pharmacist

31. El Barto
32. *Puke-A-Hontas*
33. Ned Flanders
34. The Simpsons
35. $5
36. A doughnut
37. True
38. A poncho
39. True
40. Raspberry

41. The Aztec
42. In detention at school
43. False
44. Radioactive Man
45. Bill Gates
46. 1599
47. Gymnastics
48. James Woods
49. Janey Hagstrom
50. A ship

LISA
Level Answers

QUIZ 1
Question rating: HARD

1. All three
2. No. 8
3. Rex
4. Emily Winthrop
5. *The Bloodening*
6. Eyeball stew
7. The Winfields
8. Kearney
9. Sarah
10. Mindy Simmons

11. Mr Molloy
12. Krusty the Clown
13. *Do Shut Up*
14. The Stagnant Springs Spa
15. Baking soda
16. Dr Foster
17. She is sucked into a plane's jet engine
18. June Bellamy
19. Uncle Moe's Family Feedbag
20. Heavenly Hills Mall

21. Cooder and Spud
22. 25
23. Homer
24. Jesse
25. Mr X

26. An observatory
27. Lisa Lionheart
28. A dam
29. Rommelwood
30. The Springfield Zoo

31. Ramrod or Meathook
32. Database
33. Alex Whitney
34. *The Jerry Springer Show*
35. Joan of Arc
36. Crows
37. Art
38. J. R. R. Toykins
39. Ray Patterson
40. Powersauce

41. A hamster
42. Benjamin
43. In a bag of ice
44. The Little Black Box
45. Linda and Paul McCartney
46. 300 pounds
47. 17
48. Jessica
49. He bares his bottom
50. Ashley Grant's

QUIZ 2

1. *Nsync
2. Chimpanzees
3. Focusyne

4. OmniTouch
5. Judge Constance Harm
6. Arthur Fortune

7. 300
8. A beard
9. A demolition derby
10. Woodrow

11. Danny Devito
12. Bob Arnold
13. Dr Monroe
14. Princess Kashmir
15. Jim Hope
16. L. T. Smash
17. A crane
18. Echo Canyon
19. Agnes Skinner
20. Rhinos

21. Jebediah Obediah
    Zachariah Jedediah
    Springfield
22. The Vanstar 1
23. Captain Jack
24. Miss Allbright
25. Rigel
26. It is covered with a large
    sticker
27. Baby Stinkbreath
28. He got paint on it

29. Seth or Munchie
30. $900

31. Evan Conover
32. The Australian Prime
    Minister
33. Mother
34. "Over a century
    without a slogan"
35. True
36. Chester J. Lampwick
37. Eliza and Lester
38. Hugo
39. In Homer's toolbox
40. Insert brain here

41. Tomatoes and tobacco
42. Llewellyn
43. Mr Burns
44. Double your money back
45. Matt Groening, the show's
    creator
46. *Bonestorm*
47. $10,000
48. Air conditioner
49. Springfield Wildcats
50. 666

Recent episodes
Answers

1. Pickled eggs
2. Marge
3. Bart
4. The Flanders
5. Mohican
6. A stapler
7. Homer
8. Cats
9. Elmo
10. Lenny

11. Homer
12. The Dalai Lama
13. Henry VIII
14. Lisa
15. A donkey
16. A treadmill
17. Artie Ziff
18. Krusty the Clown
19. Mozart
20. Krusty the Clown

21. Homer Simpson
22. Ray
23. Milhouse
24. Lisa
25. Groundskeeper Willie
26. Sprawlmart

27. The Lush Valley Winery
28. Ten
29. Springfield Glacier
30. Six out of ten

31. 50 Cent
32. Miss Krabappel
33. Camper Kong (a gorilla)
34. Shelbyville
35. Nelson Muntz's
36. Krusty the Clown
37. Homer
38. Mr Burns
39. Bart
40. Homer

41. Krusty the Clown
42. Chief Wiggum's
43. Injured himself with a switchblade
44. Maggie
45. Professor Stephen Hawking
46. A professional golfer
47. Comic Book Guy
48. The Red Dress Press
49. Mr Burns
50. Gravy Aficionado

QUIZ 2

1. Barney
2. Homer
3. Moe
4. Homer
5. A hot air balloon

6. Donuts
7. Ned Flanders
8. Groundskeeper Willie
9. The Serenity Ranch
10. Ralph

Recent episodes Answers

11. Homer
12. Pogo sticks
13. Dr. Hibbert
14. Gina
15. Italian
16. Giant panda
17. Kent Brockman
18. Lisa
19. Roofi
20. A belly button

21. Carl
22. Marshmallow
23. Pacman and Ms Pacman
24. Homer and Marge
25. Maude Flanders
26. Half a glass
27. US$100,000
28. Mr Burns
29. Chloe Talbot
30. Coltrane

31. Homer
32. Bart and Milhouse
33. Homer
34. Nelson Muntz
35. A skunk
36. 62 years
37. Maggie and Marge
38. Ned Flanders'
39. Chinese acrobat
40. Cinnamon

41. Homer
42. Ned Flanders
43. Two hours
44. A hammock
45. 17
46. Mr Burns
47. Bookaccino's
48. Kabul
49. Barney
50. The Harpooned Heart

172